Reweaving the Economy

How IT Affects the Borders of Country and Organization

Soichiro Takagi

University of Tokyo Press

First Edition is published on February 2017
by University of Tokyo Press.
Copyright © 2017 by Soichiro Takagi

All rights reserved. This book, or parts thereof, may not be reproduced in any form or by any means, electronic or mechanical, including photocopying, recording or any information storage and retrieval system now known or to be invented, without written permission from University of Tokyo Press.

University of Tokyo Press
4–5–29 Komaba, Meguro-ku, Tokyo 153–0041, Japan
Website: http://www.utp.or.jp/

Printed in Japan
ISBN978–4–13–047069–8

Reweaving the Economy

Foreword

Information technology (IT) pervasively affects modern society, from daily communication to business models and politics. The impact of the development of IT is also prominent on business organizations. The impact is not only about the internal structure of departments and divisions, but also about the relation between countries, regions, and entities in the market. For instance, offshore outsourcing of information services such as software development and call-center operations exemplify a new form of international production sharing. Another impact of information technology is cloud computing, which shows that it is possible to outsource computing capabilities, instead of outsourcing a whole business unit. The latest development of mass collaboration suggests that a significant part of production can be carried out by the collaboration of individuals rather than formal business entities. These organizational changes show the emergence of new relations between countries, organizations, and individuals, each of which needs to adjust its role in the market by adapting to the new environments and opportunities. In other words, information technology affects how people cooperate to produce value. Because changes in productive organizations include their impact on international trade and domestic industrial structures, these organizational changes could significantly impact the national economy as regards output, employment, and productivity.

The aim of this book is to assess the impact of information technology on the economy, through structural changes in productive organizations. In particular, this book answers questions about how the development of IT affects organizational structure for production, and how these structural changes affect the Japanese economy, in terms of employment, productivity, and output. In this analysis, most discussions are based on a Japanese context and data from Japan, but the implications can sometimes be applied universally through comparison with prior studies.

This book provides an integrated view to understanding the impact of changing organizational structures. For this purpose, analyses are conducted in stages based on a timeline from past to present. Additionally, future organizational forms are also explored to draw implications from such analyses. The analyses are reinforced by microeconomic analysis on organizational structures based on transaction cost economics, which provides the foundation for firms' decisions on organizational structure. Additionally, the analysis on national culture as a determinant of foreign direct investment in the service sector is provided to offer insights for the discussion on international production sharing of information services in the following chapters.

In the "past" stage in the integrated approach, the impact of offshore outsourcing of information services is analyzed. The analysis empirically assesses the impact of offshore outsourcing on Japanese employment from 2002 to 2006, specifying the partner countries to which information services are outsourced. Additionally, partner countries are related to certain business processes which are outsourced from Japan. The results on the impact on employment show that information services outsourcing affects employment in the manufacturing sector in Japan, but the impact is different depending on trading partners.

On the other hand, the effect of offshore outsourcing on productivity is also assessed following the same framework as the analysis on employment. The results show that the manufacturing sector gains positive effects from outsourcing to a wider range of countries than the service sector. In sum, the general impact of offshore outsourcing is the rise of productivity and the reduction of employment although the impact varies across trading partners.

In the "present" stage, cloud computing is analyzed based on

DSGE (Dynamic Stochastic General Equilibrium) analysis. This analysis identifies multiple paths through which cloud computing affects the economy, and integrates the impact through these paths. The results suggest that cloud computing can raise output and employment if productivity growth is sufficient. However, one of the reasons for the positive relation between productivity and employment in DSGE analysis may be unconstrained demand.

Since the late 2000s, collaboration between individuals has attracted increasing attention. In order to draw comprehensive implications from the results of the analyses, future development of organizational structure is also discussed. In particular, the latest development of mass collaboration is discussed related to the open data movement and the shift to an information-centric economy. This discussion illustrates how the development of IT enabled not only the collaboration between organizations, but also between individuals, and mass collaboration and outsourcing partly share common grounds in terms of the development of IT and transaction costs.

The overall findings and implications in this book are summarized as follows. First, the analyses on organizational structure suggest that business organizations are changing from a hierarchically to vertically disintegrated structure through the development of IT, through the standardization of services, and through the development of communication networks. In addition, the shift to horizontal accumulation is also observed as a result of businesses pursuing an economy of scale. Secondly, analyses on offshore outsourcing and cloud computing suggest that overcoming the downward pressure on employment is the key to benefitting from IT. Analyses showed that the impact of offshore outsourcing is the rise of productivity and the reduction of employment. On the other hand, DSGE analysis on cloud computing suggests that it is also possible to raise output and employment if productivity growth is sufficient. However, one of the reasons for the positive relation between productivity and employment in DSGE analysis may be unconstrained demand. In this sense, to realize the benefits of IT on the economy, it is important to ensure IT contributes to the development of new products or services which create new demand.

Thirdly, there are significant differences among Asian countries as trading partners in terms of the effect of offshore outsourcing on economies. For example, outsourcing to China has a positive effect both on employment and productivity. On the other hand, outsourcing to India and ASEAN 6 countries has a negative effect on manufacturing employment. These analyses on offshore outsourcing showed that there is significant diversity on the effects of the international trade of information services on the national economy depending on trading partners, even when limited to Asian countries. In this sense, considering how to realize mutually beneficial relationships with each country, instead of generalizing Asia as a trading partner is important.

Acknowledgements

This book is the revised and expanded edition of the author's Ph D dissertation entitled "Information Technology, Organization, and the Japanese Economy." In the course of composing the dissertation, I received the support of many outstanding professors. I would like to thank my academic advisor, Professor Hideyuki Tanaka, for his continuous advice and suggestions which provided great insight. I would also like to thank Professor Osamu Sudo, Professor Shigeto Sonoda, Professor Emeritus Yasuharu Ukai, and Mr. Yoshikazu Okamoto for their helpful comments. Other research and discussions from academic conferences also helped me to develop my study. I would also like to thank the faculties and students of the Graduate School of Interdisciplinary Information Studies, the University of Tokyo, for their discussions of this work and the excellent academic environment. My thanks also go to Mr. Kensuke Goto of University of Tokyo Press, for his continuous and kind support. Finally, this book would not have been realized without the support of my wife, Ai. The Japan Society for the Promotion of Science (JSPS) facilitated this book by Grant-in-Aid for Publication of Scientific Research Results (FY 2016). Chapters 3 and 5 have been partially supported by JSPS Kakenhi Grant Number 23500306. All errors remain the author's.

Contents

Figures and Tables   xi

PART I. Introduction

CHAPTER 1. The Dynamism of Information
Technology and Organization   3

   1.1 Information Technology, Organization,
and the Economy   3
   1.2 An Integrated Approach   5
   1.3 Focus on a Service and Information-
centric Economy   10
   1.4 The Structure of this Book   11

CHAPTER 2. Information Technology and
Economic Research   15

   2.1 Structure of Prior Studies   15
   2.2 IT and Economic Performance   17
   2.3 IT and Organizations   18
   2.4 Determinants of Foreign Direct
Investment in the Services Sector   21
   2.5 Empirical Analysis on the Offshore
Outsourcing of Information Services   22
   2.6 Economic Analysis of Cloud Computing   26
   2.7 Development of Mass Collaboration   29
   2.8 Conclusion   33

PART II. **Information Technology and International Production Sharing**

CHAPTER 3. Information Technology and the Organizational Structure of Modern Business Outsourcing   37

    3.1 Background   37
    3.2 Theoretical Foundation   40
    3.3 Transaction Costs and Organizational Structure   47
    3.4 Application of the Analytical Tool   50
    3.5 A Comparison of the Three Cases   56
    3.6 Conclusions   57

CHAPTER 4. Foreign Direct Investment in the Service Sector and National Culture   59

    4.1 Introduction   59
    4.2 The AsiaBarometer   60
    4.3 Methodology   61
    4.4 Results   66
    4.5 Discussion   69
    4.6 Conclusion   69

PART III. **Information Technology and the Japanese Economy**

CHAPTER 5. Offshore Outsourcing of Information Services and Employment   77

    5.1 Introduction   77
    5.2 Measurement Methodology   82
    5.3 Outsourcing Trends   85
    5.4 Estimation of the Effect on Employment   87
    5.5 Discussion   89
    5.6 Conclusion   94

CHAPTER 6. Offshore Outsourcing of Information
           Services and Productivity   99

    6.1 Introduction   99
    6.2 Trend of Variables   100
    6.3 Estimation of the Effect on TFP   101
    6.4 Discussion   106
    6.5 Conclusion   108

CHAPTER 7. Macroeconomic Analysis of Cloud
           Computing based on the
           Organizational View   113

    7.1 Background   113
    7.2 Models   115
    7.3 Results of the Impulse Response Analysis 125
    7.4 Discussion   127
    7.5 Conclusion   128

           PART IV. Future Prospects and Conclusion

CHAPTER 8. Mass Collaboration and Open
           Resources in the Information Age   139

    8.1 Open Data and Mass Collaboration   139
    8.2 Development of Open Data in Japan   141
    8.3 The Economic Rationality of Mass
        Collaboration   145
    8.4 Open Data and Regional Characteristics   147
    8.5 Implications and Future Challenges   149
    8.6 Conclusion   150

CHAPTER 9. Conclusion   153

    9.1 Key Findings of the Analyses   153
    9.2 Overall Implications   155
    9.3 Academic Implications   159

9.4 Future Challenges in an Age of
     Networked Production   160

References   163
Index   175

Figures and Tables

Figures

Figure 1–1. Stages and dimensions of analysis   7
Figure 3–1. Relationships of terms   45
Figure 3–2. Framework of outsourcing decision   45
Figure 3–3. Scope of analysis   46
Figure 3–4. Analytical tools on organizational modes   48
Figure 3–5. Organizational structure of software development   51
Figure 3–6. Organizational structure of call-center operation   53
Figure 3–7. Organizational structure of cloud computing   55
Figure 5–1. Components of information services   79
Figure 5–2. Trend of value of imports from source countries   86
Figure 5–3. Trend of share of exporting countries   86
Figure 6–1. TFP trend (1980 = 1.0)   101
Figure 7–1. Diffusion path of cloud computing   119
Figure 7–2. Relationship of endogenous variables   121
Figure 7–3. Results of the impulse response analysis on y, z, and n 126
Appendix 7–A. Impulse response analysis (Scenario 1)   131
Appendix 7–B. Impulse response analysis (Scenario 2)   132
Appendix 7–C. Impulse response analysis (Scenario 3)   133
Appendix 7–D. Impulse response analysis (Scenario 4)   134
Appendix 7–E. Impulse response with $\phi = 0.04$ 135
Figure 8–1. Mechanisms for open data to promote mass collaboration   146

Tables

Table 2–1. Major studies on IT, economic performance, and organizations   16

Figures and Tables

Table 2–2. Major studies on economic impact through organizational change	16
Table 2–3. Macroeconomic impact of cloud computing in Etro (2009, 2011)	27
Table 3–1. Comparison of the three cases on transaction costs	56
Table 4–1. Summery of statistics in variables in model 1	63
Table 4–2. Promax rotation of 3 factors of the 7 variables in the AsiaBarometer	64
Table 4–3. Summery of statistics in independent variables in model 2	64
Table 4–4. Correlations of variables	65
Table 4–5. Variable estimation of model 1	67
Table 4–6. Variable estimation of model 2	68
Appendix 4–A. Economies in the AsiaBarometer and survey year	72
Appendix 4–B. Cultural variables of countries in the AsiaBarometer	73
Table 5–1. The relation of countries and the outsourced business process	81
Table 5–2. Exporting countries and country groups in the analysis	82
Table 5–3. Results of estimation (Contemporaneous model), 2002–2006	90
Table 5–4. Results of estimation (Lagged model), 2002–2006	91
Appendix 5–A. Summery of statistics, 2002–2006	97
Appendix 5–B. Correlation matrix, 2002–2006	98
Table 6–1. Results of estimation (Contemporaneous model), 2002–2006	104
Table 6–2. Results of estimation (Lagged model), 2002–2006	105
Appendix 6–A. Summary statistics	111
Appendix 6–B. Correlation of Variables	112
Table 7–1. Calibration of structural parameters of the base model	122
Table 7–2. Calibration of operational parameters	125
Table 7–3. Calibration of ϕ	125
Table 7–4. Results at 20% diffusion of cloud computing	127

Appendix 7–F. Steady state values 136
Table 8–1. The results of analysis 148

About the Author

Soichiro Takagi is the General Manager of Research Division, Associate Professor, and Executive Research Fellow at Center for Global Communications (GLOCOM) at International University of Japan. He also serves as a Visiting Researcher at the University of Tokyo. Through his career, he also served as an Asia Program Fellow at Harvard Kennedy School, visiting researcher at SFC research institute at Keio University, and a visiting associate professor at The University of Tokyo, etc. He received Ph.D. in information studies from the University of Tokyo.

His major field is information economics, focusing on the relationship between information technology and the economy. He has examined a variety of topics including offshore outsourcing, cloud computing, open data, sharing economy, digital currency, and Blockchain. He is directing the Blockchain Economic Research Lab at GLOCOM. He has authored many books and articles, including *Methodology of Re-education: How To Go To Graduate School as Business Persons* (in Japanese). He received a SSI Best Research Award for Rising Researcher from the Society of Socio-Informatics.

PART I
Introduction

CHAPTER 1
The Dynamism of Information Technology and Organization

1.1 Information Technology, Organization, and the Economy

Information technology (IT) pervasively affects modern society, from daily communication to business models and politics. The impact of the development of IT is also prominent on business organizations. Even looking at only the last decade, the vast proliferation of smart phones and social media is affecting business and communication around the world.

The impact of the development of information technology is also prominent on business organizations. The impact is not only about the internal structure of departments and divisions, but also about the impact on the relationships between countries, regions, and entities in the market. For instance, offshore outsourcing of information services such as software development and call-center operation illustrates a new form of international production sharing. Another case is cloud computing, which shows that it is possible to outsource a computing capability, instead of outsourcing a whole business unit. The latest development of mass collaboration suggests that a significant part of production can be carried out by the collaboration of individuals, not by formal business entities. These organizational changes show the emergence of new relations between countries, organizations, and individuals, each of which needs to adjust its role in the market to new environments and opportunities. In other words, information technology affects how people cooperate to produce value.

"Organization" includes a wide range of meanings; for example, 'organization' can include social organizations such as the relation of political and economic entities, or it can include a relation between workers and incentive schemes in business firms. The term "organization" in this study generally refers to business organizations, focusing on how business processes for producing value are carried out. Specifically, it focuses on the scope of productive capabilities and the relation between those who take part in producing value.

There are prior studies on the impact of IT on organizations, but linking organizational change with macroeconomic analysis is not an easy task (Brynjolfsson and Hitt 2000). Such difficulty, in part, arises where prior studies focus on intra-firm management issues as the major organizational topics associated with information technology. For example, Bresnahan et al. (2002) assessed the relation between IT and intra-firm management such as team-based work organization, individual decision authority, and skills and education. Incorporating these elements into a macroeconomic framework is difficult because these organizational characteristics are absorbed with other elements into firm-level performance.

This book focuses on the boundary and external relationship of organizations rather than focusing on intra-firm management. These boundary and external relationships typically include issues on outsourcing, and are more directly related to industrial structure and the composition of the national economy. From the perspective of prior studies on organizations and macroeconomics, this book tries to link organizational structures and macroeconomics by focusing on the boundary and external relationship of productive organizations.

Because these changing relations of productive organizations include the impact on international trade and domestic industrial structure, they can significantly impact the national economy in terms of output, employment, and productivity. The aim of this research is to assess the impact of IT on the economy, through the structural changes in productive organization. In particular, this research will answer questions about how the development of IT affects the organizational structure for production, and how these structural changes affect the Japanese economy, such as employment and productivity. In the course of analysis, most of the discussions are based on Japanese contexts and data, but implications are drawn occasionally for universal application through comparison with prior studies.

The rest of this introductory chapter explains the approach needed to achieve this research goal. The approach of this book is discussed through two points of view: an integrated approach and a focus on service and an information-centric economy. The following discussion on these approaches clarifies the structure of the research and the characteristics of this book.

1.2 An Integrated Approach

The impact of information technology on organizational structure can take various forms, such as the international outsourcing of information services, adoption of cloud computing, and mass collaboration. This study tries to provide an integrated view on these multiple phenomena, based on a common analytical foundation and assessment on the impact of each type of organizational change on the economy. In particular, the integrated approach of this study is characterized by three points: analysis through dynamic change of organizational form, integration of the macro and microeconomic approach, and methodological diversity such as industry level evidence and the DSGE analysis.

Analysis through dynamic change of organizational form

This research views the development of IT as affecting the organizational structure of productive activities, and this change in organizational structure is continuously ongoing because of the ceaseless development of IT. Therefore, one of the important points in this book is analysis and discussion based on these dynamically changing organizational changes.

This research covers mainly offshore outsourcing of information services and cloud computing, and also complements the argument on the effect of these two organizational changes by discussing mass collaboration. These organizational changes are emerging consecutively along with a timeline, but also emerging as a consequence of technological development. Arthur (2009, p. 110) argues that there are two patterns in invention: one which starts from a perceived need then finds a principle, and the other which starts from phenomenon and then finds a principle of use. This research mainly considers technological developments as enablers for the emergence of a certain organizational structure. However, these organizational changes are also discussed from the demand side complementarily in the final chapter.

The other important point in Arthur (2009) is that new technologies must arise by combination of existing technologies (p. 19), and that accumulation of technologies leads to more accumulation (p. 20). In the field of IT, available technologies are drastically increasing, which in turn serve as the building blocks of new technology, and accelerate innovation in the IT field. Therefore, if organizational structure is also affected by the available technology,[1] the change in organizational adjustment can be diverse and also accelerate. To understand the effect of IT on organizations and the economy, it is not sufficient to analyze only one of these organizational changes because each organizational form might be one of the representations of continuous change. Instead, it is important to identify the mechanisms by which IT affects organizational structure, and discuss how the economy is affected by the continuous change of organizations.

To provide an integrated view to understanding these changing organizational structures, analyses are conducted on stages based on a timeline which characterizes the past, present, and future of organizational change (Figure 1–1). As discussed above, these organizational changes emerge approximately along with time, but these changes also reflect the order of the emergence of technologies

---

[1] Arthur (2009) argues that organizations can be also one of the technologies in a certain aspect.

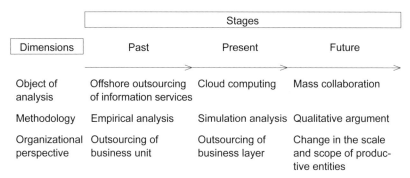

Figure 1-1. Stages and dimensions of analysis

which enable these organizational forms to become available.

In the "past" stage, offshore outsourcing of information services is set as an objective of analysis. Since the early 2000s, the development of information technology and communication networks has made various services tradable, such as software development and call-center operations. Since then, offshore outsourcing of these services has been conducted globally with a significant continuity. Given the availability of data on outsourcing transactions, this analysis is conducted based on empirical and quantitative analysis. In particular, the impacts on employment and productivity are examined. From an organizational economics perspective, offshore outsourcing is considered an organization to organization outsourcing of a certain business unit across borders.

For the "present" stage, cloud computing is set as the objective of study. Since the middle of 2000s, cloud computing has become one of the major topics among information technology architecture, but its effect on the economy is not known well. Because empirical data on the transactions of cloud computing is not fully available, this analysis is conducted as a simulation based on DSGE (Dynamic Stochastic General Equilibrium) analysis. From an organizational perspective, cloud computing is considered the outsourcing of a common layer of business, because computing resources are used by various business units such as sales management, human resources management, and financial management.

In terms of the "future" stage, the collaboration of individuals for productive activity has attracted attention since the late 2000s, with the emergence of open source software or the online encyclopedia. One of the symbolic terms to describe this phenomenon is crowdsourcing, which is characterized by the combination of a top-down outsourcing approach and the participation of mass individuals (Brabham 2012). These collaborations are still in an initial stage of emerging phenomena and not a major component of the economy. However, if this collaboration has an economic rationality as productive organizations, it can be viewed as one of the future developments of organizational structure. As discussed in this chapter, this study views organizational change as continuously ongoing because of the ceaseless development of IT. In order to draw implications from the results of the analyses, it would be worthwhile to explore the future development of organizational structure. Therefore, the future development of organizational structure is also discussed. Particularly, the latest development of mass collaboration is discussed in relation to the 'open data movement' and the shift to an information-centric economy. This book also argues for the economic rationality of mass collaboration and its relation to outsourcings. The overall implication of this research is drawn based on the analysis on offshore outsourcing and cloud computing, taking into account the argument on future organizational development.

Integration of macro and microeconomic approach

The ultimate goal of this study is to assess the impact of information technology on the economy on a macroeconomic scale. However, the study is also based on the microeconomic foundations of an entity's decisions regarding its own activities. There are various ways to make research more comprehensive by including multilevel analysis, such as including industry level and firm level analysis (e.g. Motohashi 2005, Ukai 2005). It is also possible to include quantitative analysis and case studies on specific firms, but in this research, the transaction cost economics (TCE) approach is employed to provide a microeconomic foundation on the economic rationality of multiple phenomena.

The analysis using TCE clarifies how the development of IT has affected organizational structure, in the form of offshore outsourcing of software development, business process outsourcing, and cloud computing. This argument is supplemented by analysis on how the cultural characteristics of a country affect the inflow of foreign direct investment in the services sector, because production sharing in information services often crosses national borders.

Additionally, the analysis on the impact of cloud computing is conducted using the DSGE (Dynamic Stochastic General Equilibrium) model. One of the main purposes of the DSGE approach is to incorporate an entity's behavior into a macroeconomics framework. Application of the DSGE approach in this study is also one of the expressions of macro and microeconomic integration. Rather than directly assessing the relations between macroeconomic variables, the microeconomic foundation in this book makes it possible to draw more in-depth findings and discussions on the impact of IT on the economy.

Methodological diversity

As introduced in this section, this book covers several topics, from offshore outsourcing, cloud computing, to mass collaboration. The most appropriate methodologies are employed in each analysis based on the objective of analysis and the available resources. For example, analysis on offshore outsourcing is based on regression analysis based on industry-level panel data. In addition, analysis on cloud computing is conducted as a simulation based on DSGE analysis. Mass collaboration is discussed qualitatively based on transaction cost economics and the description of the latest development practices of mass collaboration and open data.

Using various methodologies, analyses on each topic fill in missing points on prior studies in each field, which are clarified in Chapter 2. Additionally, analyses on each topic complement each other because the scope and the depth of analysis differ depending on the object of analysis and methodologies. This diversity of methodology plays an important role in drawing integrated implications from findings and in discussing the current academic frontier, as well as in the challenges for economic analysis on the information economy. These implications and challenges are discussed in the final chapter.

1.3 Focus on a Service and Information-centric Economy

This study is based on a viewpoint that focuses on the shift towards service and an information-centric economy. In terms of the scope of analysis, this study focuses on the impact of organizational change for specifically providing "information services" because information services are becoming an important component of economy, and also because organizations for providing information services are most affected by the development of information technology. The impact of organizational change for providing information services on the economy are assessed by dividing the effects of the impact to the manufacturing and service sector in Chapters 5 and 6, while Chapter 7 assesses the impact of organizational change on the entire economy.

Information services have characteristics such as "information" and "services", both of which have unique characteristics and importance when analyzing the modern economy. The service sector is increasingly becoming a major component in the economy, and the service sector has unique characteristics such as heterogeneity and proximity with customers. As the economy becomes more composed of the service sector, the decision on the boundary of firms and trade is affected by these characteristics as services. This relation of service attributes and organizational structure is discussed in Chapter 3 in detail.

On the other hand, "information" also has a unique characteristic as an object of trade. While Benkler (2006) suggests that economy is more centered on information production, Noguchi (1974) discusses the characteristics of information as economic goods, such as the cost for copy and the value of information. These points on the characteristics of information are discussed in detail in the final chapter.

This research is based on integrated analysis from past and present to the future, and the focus on the shift to service and an information-centric economy. These approaches clarify how information technology not only affects the boundaries of firms, but also affects how value is created through the relationship of entities.

1.4 The Structure of this Book

This book consists of four parts. Part I is the introductory section containing this chapter and Chapter 2, which is the literature review and introduces prior studies for the analyses in this book. Specifically, Chapter 2 assesses how prior studies handled information technology and organizational issues in the studies on economy in terms both of the general framework and of specific topics. In general, most prior studies provide snapshots of limited phenomena on the impact of information technology on the economy. However, the analysis based on the overarching framework of the dynamically changing practice of IT and organizational structure is missing. Additionally, the literature review also suggests that prior studies on specific topics are also in initial stages, and there are a lot of missing points.

Part II provides a discussion on the relation between IT and organizational structure. Chapter 3 discusses the microeconomic framework on organizational structure, which constitutes the foundation of the following analyses. This chapter analyzes the mechanisms behind a firm's decision on the outsourcing of information services, using transaction cost economics and service attributes. The discussion shows how the development of information technology affects organizational structure, and the difference of a firms' decisions on several objective services, such as software development, business process outsourcing, and cloud computing. Based on this foundation of a firm's decisions on organizational structure, analyses on economic impact are discussed along with dynamic change in the development of IT and organizational structure.

Chapter 4 provides analysis on the determinants of international production sharing in the service sector, one of which is information services. Because acceptance of foreign services is influenced by national culture in host countries, national culture is analyzed as a key determinant for FDI inflow, with a comparison of different impacts in service and non-service sectors.

Part III discusses the results of quantitative analysis on how IT affects the Japanese economy. Chapters 5 and 6 analyze the "past" stage, i.e., the impact of offshore outsourcing of information services, which is assessed empirically based on a regression analysis of industry-level panel data. The analysis specifies the partner countries of offshore outsourcing and outsourced business processes, assessing the impact on employment in Chapter 5, and the impact on productivity in Chapter 6. These analyses discuss the impact based on the results of empirical analyses and the mechanisms for the decision on organizational structure which is discussed in Part II.

In the "present" stage, cloud computing is analyzed in Chapter 7 based on DSGE analysis, which is a simulation analysis on macroeconomic variables when the economy encounters the diffusion of cloud computing. Whereas empirical analysis on the past stage directly assesses the relation between the amount of offshore outsourcing and employment or productivity, the DSGE analyses on the present stage is based on mathematical models which define microeconomic entities such as firms and households, and the analyses assess the impact on comprehensive variables on a macroeconomic scale. This analysis identifies multiple paths through which cloud computing affects the economy, and integrates the impact through these paths. The discussion on the implication is also based on the perception of organizational structure in Chapter 3.

Part IV discusses the latest developments of organizational structure and provides the conclusion to this book. For the "future" stage, Chapter 8 describes the latest movement of open data, which is stimulating the emergence of mass collaboration in Japan. In particular, how open data is enabling mass collaboration is examined in this chapter, because the mechanisms behind the emergence of mass collaboration are beyond the initial scope of analysis on organizational structure in Chapter 3. In this sense, the discussion on economic rationality on mass collaboration is an extension of the initial discussion on organizational structure in Chapter 3. Chapter 8 describes the movement of open data and mass collaboration in Japan with analyses on how open data is associated with mass collaboration from the viewpoint of organizational economics. The discussion will show that the development of information technology affects not only the relations of business organizations, but also the scale and scope of entities for production and the relation between them. Additionally, this chapter also provides the results of preliminary analysis on how the regional characteristics of municipalities affect the decision of local governments to conduct open data initiatives.

After the discussion on mass collaboration in Chapter 8, overall findings and implications are summarized through three points in Chapter 9. First, the analyses on organizational structure suggest that business organizations are changing from a hierarchy to a vertically disintegrated form through the standardization of services and the development of communication networks. In addition, the shift to horizontal accumulation is also observed as the result of seeking a scale economy. Secondly, results of analyses suggest that the impact of offshore outsourcing on the economy through organizational change is generally the rise of productivity and the reduction of employment. Cloud computing could raise output and employment if productivity growth is sufficient, but it is only feasible when demand is not constrained. Therefore, overcoming the downward pressure on employment is the key to benefit from information technology, and demand creation is important for the solution. Thirdly, Asian countries show significant variety as trading partners regarding the effect of offshore outsourcing on the economy. Therefore, it is important to consider how to realize mutually beneficial relationships with each country instead of generalizing Asia as a single trading partner. Chapter 9 also discusses the limits, academic contribution, and future challenges of this book.

CHAPTER 2
Information Technology and Economic Research

This chapter reviews prior studies which cover the topics of this book. A wide range of prior studies are related to this book; therefore, the structure of prior studies is presented first. Based on the structure, prior studies are discussed in categories such as IT and productivity or firm value, IT and organizations, offshore outsourcing, and cloud computing.

A review of prior studies reveals that most prior studies provide snapshots on the limited phenomena of the impact of information technology on the economy, but the analyses from the viewpoint of dynamically changing IT and organization is insufficient. Additionally, the review of prior studies also suggests that prior studies on the specific topics addressed in this book are also in initial stages, and there are many missing points.

2.1 Structure of Prior Studies

The structure of major prior studies is presented in Tables 2–1 and 2–2 with the chapters of this book. Studies in Table 2–1 are those which assess the direct impact of information technology on economic performance and organizations. Most of these studies assess the impact of IT on productivity, and some studies assess the impact on firm value and employment. Studies in Table 2–2 assess the impact of information technology through organizational changes, such as the form of offshore outsourcing or cloud computing. These studies are categorized by locations, such as the U.S. and Europe, and Asia. The remaining part of this chapter introduces and discusses the prior studies based on these structures.

Table 2–1. Major studies on IT, economic performance, and organizations

Topics		Studies
IT and economic performances	The U.S. and Europe	Solow (1987), Brynjolfsson (1993), Oliner and Sichel (1994), Brynjolfsson and Hitt (1996), Jorgenson and Stiroh (1999), Siegel (1997), Oliner and Sichel (2000), Jorgenson et al. (2011)
	Japan	Jorgenson and Motohashi (2003), Motohashi (2005), Matsudaira (1998), Takemura (2003), Minetaki and Nishimura (2010), Ukai and Watanabe (2001), Ukai and Takemura (2001)
IT and organizations	IT and intra-firm management	Hitt (1999), Brynjolfsson et al. (1994), Hitt and Brynjolfsson (1997), Coase (1937), Williamson (1983), Dibbern et al. (2008), Ang and Straub (1998), Bahli and Rivard (2003), Blair et al. (2011), Bresnahan et al. (2002), Keizai-kikakucho (2000)
	IT and the external relationship of organizations	Chapters 3 and 4 of this book

Note: The shaded area is the focus of this study.

Table 2–2. Major studies on economic impact through organizational change

Topics	The U.S. and Europe	Asia	
		Japan	Estimation with a variety of Asian economies
Offshore outsourcing	Liu and Trefler (2008), Amiti and Wei (2005, 2009), Falk and Wolfmayr (2008)	Chapters 5 and 6 of this book	
Cloud computing	Etro (2009, 2011)	Chapter 7 of this book Tamegawa et al. (2014), Ukai (2013), Ukai and Inagaki (2014)	
Mass collaboration	Tapscott and Williams (2008), Howe (2009), Brabham (2012), Estellés-Arolas and González-Ladrón-de-Guevara (2012), Gurin (2014)	Chapter 8 of this book	

Note: Shaded areas are the focus of this study.

2.2 IT and Economic Performance

Since the surging development and proliferation of information technology, its impact has raised a wide range of public concern. During the early development of information technology and the Internet in the 1980s, positive expectations for economic growth have been characterized by the term, the "new economy." These expectations have been realized as a number of startups which resulted in a large number of businesses in software, networks, and information services.

From an economic viewpoint, the central question on the development of information technology has been whether the utilization of IT could contribute to the rise of productivity. Watanabe and Ukai (2003), who provide an overarching review on the literature and have studied extensively the economic and business impact of information technology, suggest that the target of academic discussion in the 1980s was the relation between IT and productivity. Motohashi (2005) also suggests that the effect of IT on productivity is the central topic of the "new economy" in the U.S.

Major prior studies which assess the direct impact of IT on economic performances including productivity and firm value, are shown in Table 2-1. A "productivity paradox" was reported in the late 1980s that noted information technology investment did not raise productivity (Solow 1987, Brynjolfsson 1993, Oliner and Sichel 1994). However, a positive effect of IT on growth has been reported gradually since the late 1990s, such as in Brynjolfsson and Hitt (1996), Jorgenson and Stiroh (1999), Siegel (1997), and Oliner and Sichel (2000). Additionally, continuous positive effects on productivity in the 2000s have been reported by Jorgenson et al. (2011). In terms of the Japanese economy, Jorgenson and Motohashi (2003) show that the growth of TFP was 1.13% from 1995 to 2000 including the contribution of IT investment. Specific effects of information technology have been assessed by Motohashi (2005), and show that Japanese firms during 1991 to 2000, which utilized information networks, mostly achieved higher TFP growth than those without information networks. Positive results of economic impact have also been reported in various articles although the significance and the size of the impact are diverse across empirical settings and in analyzed industrial sectors (e.g. Matsudaira 1998, Takemura 2003). Minetaki and Nishimura (2010) provide analyses on the impact of information technology on the Japanese economy from various aspects such as labor and productivity. Their analyses include the relation between outsourcing and productivity in the Japanese information services industry at the firm level in 1990s although their analysis does not focus on outsourcing overseas.

On the other hand, there are studies which assess the impact on firm value in financial markets. Ukai and Watanabe (2001) showed that both hardware and software stock led to higher firm value in Japanese banking firms in the late 1990s, and Ukai and Takemura (2001) showed that only software stocks also contributed to higher firm value during 1993 to 1999 for the same industry.

2.3 IT and Organizations

There are also prior studies which discuss the relation between the utilization of information technology and organizations, as seen in Table 2–2. Among them, there are several studies which assess the impact of IT on organizations quantitatively at the firm level. For example, Hitt (1999) assessed the relations between IT capital and the boundary of firms using firm-level panel data analysis, and found that more IT capital is associated with vertical disintegration and more diversification. Brynjolfsson et al. (1994) examined the relation between IT capital and firm size, and found that greater IT capital is associated with a decrease in the firm size. Hitt and Brynjolfsson (1997) assessed the relations between IT capital and the internal organization of firms. They found that greater IT capital is associated with organizations with decentralized authority.

However, relating these organizational changes with macroeconomic variables is not sufficient. Brynjolfsson and Hitt (2000) suggest that there is a substantial amount of literature on the impact of IT on organizations, outputs, and productivity at the firm level. However, they state that these effects are "not well captured by traditional macroeconomic measurement approaches" and one of the reasons is that assumptions are needed to "incorporate complementary organizational factors into a growth accounting framework" (Brynjolfsson and Hitt 2000, p. 25).

One of the difficulties in linking organizational issues with macroeconomic variables arises where there are too many aspects to the term "organization" even when limiting the scope to business organizations. For example, Bresnahan et al. (2002) assessed the relation between IT and elements such as team-based work organization, individual decision authority, and skills and education. Their study was referred to by other studies including Keizai-kikakucho (2000), which studied similar research on Japan. Keizai-kikakucho (2000) focused on the decentralization of organizations, such as self-management teams, flat management, and teamwork in promotions. Black and Lynch (2004) did not specifically assess the relation between IT and organizations, but they suggested that workplace innovations such as incentive schemes for employee were one of the contributors for increasing productivity in the new economy. These studies focused on intra-firm aspects such as the capability of workers and the relationship between them. However, incorporating these elements into a macroeconomic framework (Brynjolfsson and Hitt 2000) is difficult because these organizational characteristics are absorbed into other elements at firm-level performance.

In contrast, this book focuses on the boundary and external relationship of productive capabilities rather than intra-firm management. These boundary and external relationships, typically issues on outsourcing, are more directly related to industrial structure and the composition of the national economy. From the perspective of prior studies on organizations and macroeconomics, this book tries to link organizational structures and macroeconomic analysis by focusing on the boundary and external relationships of productive organizations.

The boundary of firms has been discussed here mainly from an organizational economics view, particularly based on transaction cost economics (TCE). TCE theorizes the boundary and the structure of firms (Coase 1937, Williamson 1983). Particularly for decisions on outsourcing, TCE is referred to as a starting point in various articles such as Willcocks and Lacity (1995), Ono and Stango (2005), and Michael and Michael (2011). Several articles for practitioners also refer to TCE as affecting the success of outsourcing projects (Kennedy and Sharma 2009, Manning 2006). A detailed discussion on the contents of transaction cost economics is provided in the analysis in Chapter 3.

On the other hand, in-depth analyses of TCE regarding the outsourcing of information services are not as abundant. Among the few studies, Dibbern et al. (2008) identified the extra costs that arise in outsourcing projects in addition to the direct costs paid to vendors, and the authors analyzed the extra costs using TCE and a knowledge-based view of firms. From case studies, they showed that the extra costs are different across each project because of different conditions such as client-specific knowledge, absorptive capacity, and geographic and cultural distance.

Ang and Straub (1998) empirically analyzed the determinants of the outsourcing of information systems and showed that transaction costs affect outsourcing decisions, but the effect of such costs is much smaller than production costs. Bahli and Rivard (2003) identified the risks concerning information services outsourcing such as lock-in, and discussed the issues from TCE and agency theory. Blair et al. (2011) focused on modularity and examined the contracts that determine the interface between vendor and buyer, although they did not focus on information services outsourcing.

These prior studies discussed TCE to estimate the true cost of the outsourcing of information services. From the beginning, these studies viewed the outsourcing of information services as possible. However, how information technology enabled services such as software development, call center operations, or computing services to become tradable is not fully discussed. The differences in decisions on organizational structure when conducting these services have not been specifically discussed in prior studies but they are essential in understanding how information technology affects organizational structure. Chapter 3 focuses on this point and analyzes the mechanisms behind outsourcing decisions by focusing on service attributes and transaction cost economics.

2.4 Determinants of Foreign Direct Investment in the Services Sector

In this section, prior studies on the determinants of FDI are summarized and discussed. Numerous empirical studies support traditional factors, such as economic growth, market size, agglomeration effects, and wage rates as key determinants of FDI inflow (e.g., Kravis and Lipsey, 1988; Milner and Pentecost, 1996). However, traditional factors are not sufficient to explain the factors necessary to determine FDI (Biswas 2002). Therefore, in addition to traditional factors, various nontraditional variables have also been examined as determinants of FDI. For example, Biswas (2002) examined nontraditional factors and found that infrastructure, low wages, property rights protection, and democracy are also important in attracting FDI. Henisz (2000) analyzed the entry mode of MNCs and found that contractual hazards lead to majority-owned entry and political hazards lead to joint-venture entry.

More recently, studies on the specific factors impacting FDI in specific regions or sectors have been explored. For example, international trade agreements (Buthe and Milner 2008), environmental regulation in China (Zhang and Fu 2008), regional conditions in China, and the location choice of Japanese MNCs (Wakasugi 2005) have been examined. However, studies on the impact of cultural factors on FDI are relatively limited. Jones and Teegen (2001) studied national culture and global R&D investments of U.S. MNCs using Hofstede's dataset to represent national culture. They found that cultural similarity between source and host country and individualism in the host country have a positive effect on R&D investments. Gao (2005) suggested that language commonality increases FDI flow in China.

However, to the author's knowledge, prior studies have not fully explored the different impact of national culture on different industrial sectors.

2.5 Empirical Analysis on the Offshore Outsourcing of Information Services

This book assesses the impact on the economy following dynamic changes from the past, present, and future. In the "past" stage, the impact of offshore outsourcing of information services on the economy is empirically assessed. The prior studies directly related to this topic are shown in Table 2-2. However, because the offshore outsourcing of information services is a form of international production sharing, this topic is placed in the field of international economics, particularly outsourcing and production sharing. Therefore, prior studies in the international economics field are introduced before discussing the studies in Table 2-2.[1]

Among the theoretical studies on production sharing, Markusen et al. (1996) argue that the similarity or difference of countries such as size, factor endowments, and trade costs characterizes the form of foreign direct investment, for example, horizontal or vertical direct investment. Other scholars have also developed theories to explain outsourcing, such as Markusen (2005), Rodriguez-Clare (2007), Baldwin and Robert-Nicoud (2007), Mitra and Ranjan (2007).

In terms of empirical studies on production sharing, a number of analyses have been conducted to assess the effect of outsourcing on the domestic economy. Since the 1980s, there has been an increasing wage gap between skilled and unskilled labor in the U.S. (Feenstra and Hanson 1999). Outsourcing has been analyzed as a factor

---

[1] This section is based on Takagi and Tanaka (2010), which has been revised and reconstructed for this book.

of this change in wages and employment. For example, Feenstra and Hanson (1997) showed that the relative demand for skilled labor increased both in developed and developing countries by production sharing. Feenstra and Hanson (2003) empirically assessed whether technological change or trade of intermediate input has affected the wage gap between skilled and unskilled labor, and concluded that both outsourcing and expenditure on computers and other high-technology capital are important explanations of the shift towards nonproduction labor in the U.S.

However, empirical results of the impact on wage and employment have not been consistent among studies. Anderton and Brenton (1999) suggested imports from low-wage countries had the effect of reducing the wage-bill share and the relative employment of less-skilled labor in the UK. On the other hand, Arndt (1998) showed that because of the outsourcing of labor-intensive components, wages rose and industry employment and output increased. Berman et al. (1994) showed that the shift towards skilled labor in the U.S. was mainly caused by technological change, not by trade. Harrison and McMillan (2006) argued that the effect on employment in the U.S. differs depending on whether the outsourcing is horizontal or vertical production sharing. Kravis and Lipsey (1988) suggested that foreign direct investment in manufacturing and the service sector have a different effect on the domestic demand of skilled labor.

On the other hand, there is another approach to economic analysis on outsourcing, which is to assess the determinants of outsourcing and the choice between foreign direct investment and outsourcing. Hanson et al. (2003) examine variables that raise demand for imported inputs. Bartel et al. (2005) studied the elements to promote IT-service trade, and showed that technological changes increased outsourcing of IT-based services. Chen et al. (2008) analyzed the importance of knowledge capital and its effect on the choice between FDI and outsourcing. Grossman and Helpman (2002b) also explored the effects of economic variables on the choice between FDI or outsourcing. Grossman and Helpman (2002a) examined the elements which affect the location choices of global production.

However, prior studies on information services trade or general service trade are very limited. Markusen (2005) pointed out that the important theoretical themes on offshoring are (a) vertical fragmentation of production, (b) expansion of trade at an extensive margin, (c) fragments that differ in factor intensities and countries that differ in endowments, and (d) knowledge or capital stocks of countries or firms that are complementary as to skilled labor and create missing inputs for countries otherwise well suited to skill-intensive fragments. Mitra and Ranjan (2007) examined the effect of offshoring on employment theoretically, and suggested that the effect depends on the allowance of labor mobility across sectors.

There are several studies on the empirical analyses of the outsourcing of information services, as seen in Table 2–2. Among them, Liu and Trefler (2008) assessed the impact of information services outsourcing to China and India on U.S. employment, while Amiti and Wei (2005) assessed UK employment and information service outsourcing, and Falk and Wolfmayr (2008) conducted similar research on the EU countries. As these three are representative works on this topic, these studies are explained in detail in this section.

Liu and Trefler (2008) deal with not only offshoring but also "inshoring" from China and India, which refers to service export from U.S. to those countries. They show that offshore outsourcing increases, and inshoring reduces the chance of job switching. They argue that the inshoring effect is much larger, therefore, for the economy as a whole and service trade reduces job switching. In terms of unemployment, they analyzed the net effect of inshoring and offshoring and argue that the service trade has a very small effect in reducing the time of unemployment. However, generally, when offshore outsourcing increases, inshoring reduces the period of unemployment. In other words, it is inferred that developed countries need sufficient export to offset the negative effect of service outsourcing in order to maintain their current industrial structure.

Amiti and Wei (2005) estimated the effect on UK employment by separating the manufacturing and service sectors. The result is that service outsourcing[2] has a positive effect on employment in the manufacturing sector. On the other hand, service outsourcing has a negative effect on employment in the service sector. However, Amiti and Wei stated that the analysis on the service sector is not robust because of the inconsistent results across specifications and a relatively limited number of cases.

Falk and Wolfmayr (2008) showed that the import of services from both low-wage and high-wage countries has no significant effect on employment in the manufacturing sector in several EU countries. Instead, they find that materials import has a negative impact on employment. In the service sector, service import from low-wage countries has a negative effect on employment. As the authors pointed out, this result is consistent with Amiti and Wei (2005), which suggested that service outsourcing might have a negative effect on employment in the service sector. But they suggest this effect is not significant when they focus on "business services."

In addition to these three works, Ebenstein et al. (2009) studied the effect of offshoring on U.S. wages and employment using individual data, and van Welsum and Reif (2006) empirically studied the factors affecting offshoring by assessing the effect on clerical and non-clerical workers separately. However, assessment on the effect of offshore outsourcing on productivity is more limited. Only Amiti and Wei (2009) have directly analyzed this point and found that offshore outsourcing of services has a positive effect on total factor productivity (TFP) in the United States.

In terms of the analyses on Japan, a series of studies by the author, such as Takagi and Tanaka (2012b, 2012c), assess the effect of the outsourcing of information services on employment and productivity in Japan. Nonetheless, these studies do not specify the

---
2 Amiti and Wei (2005) focus on computing and information and other business services.

partner countries or outsourced business processes.

In sum, there are two missing points in prior studies on this topic. First, empirical analyses have been conducted on the U.S., the UK, and EU countries, but analysis on Japan has not been sufficient. To study this topic further, Japan, with its unique characteristics such as its economic network in East Asia, employment regulations and structures, and the multi-layer outsourcing in its information technology industry should also be included. Moreover, prior studies do not analyze the variety of the effects of information services outsourcing depending on the unique Asian trading partners. Chapters 5 and 6 fill in these missing points by conducting the analysis on Japan.

2.6 Economic Analysis of Cloud Computing

The "present" stage of organizational change is cloud computing. A large number of articles have been published on cloud computing, but its concerns and academic disciplines have been scattered across the literature. For example, some studies focus on technological architecture (e.g. Cretu 2012, Endo et al. 2011), and others discuss security and privacy issues (e.g. Anthes 2010, Qaisar and Khawaja 2012, Reddy and Reddy 2011). Some studies also discuss market governance such as competition law and regulation (Durkee 2010, Strømmen-Bakhtiar and Razavi 2011).

On the other hand, an analytical framework and methodology for macroeconomic analyses have been developed in the last decade. Emerging from the analysis of the fluctuation of the business cycle (Kydland and Prescott 1982, Long and Plosser 1983), macroeconomic analysis with a micro-foundation has become one of the dominant schools in economic literature. However, even though one of the major concerns of the basic RBC model has been on technological innovation, RBC and DSGE have been developed focusing mainly on monetary and financial analysis. More recently, DSGE analysis started to be applied to a wider range of topics such as the effect of immigration (Mandelman and Zlate 2008), incor-

Table 2–3. Macroeconomic impact of cloud computing in Etro (2009, 2011)

	Speed of diffusion	Short term	Medium term	Unit
GDP	Slow	+0.05	+0.1	Percentage points per year
	Rapid	+0.15	+0.3	
Business Creation	Slow	+73,256	+83,478	Number of firms per year
	Rapid	+378,640	+430,973	
Job Creation	Slow	+300,000	+70,000	Number of workers per year
	Rapid	+1,000,000 or more	+700,000	

Notes: The impact on GDP and business creation is taken from Etro (2009), and the impact on job creation is from Etro (2011). Source: Etro (2009) and Etro (2011)

poration of on-the-job searches (Macit 2010), productivity and energy prices (Dhawan et al. 2008).

However, assessment of the economic impacts of cloud computing are limited as can be seen in Table 2–2. Etro (2009, 2011) uses a DSGE approach on cloud computing. These studies have focused on the cost reduction effect of cloud computing and have analyzed its macroeconomic impact based on the DSGE model. The underlying perception of these studies is that cloud computing turns information technology costs from fixed costs to marginal costs of production. These studies assume first that the cost reduction of IT investment lowers the initial barrier of entry for new firms and fosters the establishment of small and medium size enterprises (SME). Second, these studies also assume that the increase of SME should have a positive effect on employment and GDP. Third, such studies also analyzed the impact on public accounts arguing that public spending is lowered and tax income is increased by the diffusion of cloud computing. Etro (2009, 2011) constructed a model augmented with an increased number of firms, and conducted a simulation of EU countries. The results show that the diffusion of cloud computing boosts GDP by 0.05% to 0.15% in the short term, and 0.1% to 0.3% in the medium term. The estimates on business creation and job creation are shown in Table 2–3.

Etro (2009, 2011) draws implications for various aspects such as GDP, business creation, and job creation, but the basic idea is that cloud computing lowers entry costs and promotes entrepreneurship. The models of these studies are developed by incorporating an endogenous growth model, but it is not easy to expand to include other aspects because of its specialized development on entry costs. More recently, Tamegawa et al. (2014) conducted DSGE analysis on cloud computing, and found that a 10 percent adoption rate of cloud computing has led to a 10 percent upward shift of production function for Japanese firms.

In addition to the analysis with the DSGE model, Ukai (2013) has analyzed the relation between the financial condition of firms and their choice of using public cloud computing, private cloud computing, or hybrid cloud computing. Ukai (2013) found paradoxical results in which firms with more assets use public cloud computing, whereas firms with high profits use a less hybrid cloud computing. Ukai and Inagaki (2014) conducted a similar analysis at the firm level, and found that Japanese firms increase the use of private cloud computing when reducing profit.

In terms of the benefit of cloud computing, Cudanov et al. (2011) pointed out flexible scalability. They argued that traditional IT investment does not meet the actual demand of ICT because it is difficult to forecast future demand perfectly, and investment is conducted once at a certain time, and not on a daily basis. Because of this gap in demand and investment, excessive investment happens under low demand, and opportunity loss happens under high demand periods. Cudanov et al. (2011) did not present the ways to measure the amount of these losses, but this flexibility would be one of the benefits of cloud computing.

On the impact on employment, Ross (2011) discussed the impact on ICT workers in user firms. From user firms' point of view, the introduction of cloud computing is similar to outsourcing because these firms utilize the resources outside the firms. Ross (2011, p. 69) argues that along with the transition from in-house operation to utilization of cloud computing, the role of ICT workers shifts from "a technical to more of a liaison role as they engage with external service providers."

As seen in this section, several studies provide perspectives on the effect of cloud computing, but they only choose various aspects partially, and do not present a comprehensive view. There are also missing points in previous studies such as the negative effect of reduced revenue for domestic ICT firms. For example, Japanese firms may import foreign cloud services instead of utilizing domestic services. Bayrak et al. (2011) also provides a literature survey on cloud computing and points out that the literature on the topic is scarce.

Economic analysis of cloud computing is in its initial stages and there is still a large opportunity for research. Chapter 7 constructs a model to incorporate the multiple effects of cloud computing, and thus provides a basis for the macroeconomic analysis of technological innovations such as cloud computing.

2.7 Development of Mass Collaboration

Analysis on the "Future" stage mentioned in this book discusses the collaboration between organizations and collaboration between smaller units of production, typically individuals. Studies on the collaboration between small units of production have evolved around the term "mass collaboration" and "crowdsourcing." This section introduces these major concepts and related studies on collaboration, and discusses the missing points and opportunities for future study.

Tapscott and Williams (2008) focus on the trend in which IT enabled individuals to participate in economic activities and calls this trend, mass collaboration. They suggest four principles for mass collaboration; namely, openness, peering, sharing, and global action. By openness, they mean innovation which collaborates with outside capabilities, the standardization of information technology, transparency of firms, and educational materials and opportunities. In contrast with hierarchical organizations, the peering emphasizes individuals who participate in economic activities, and the authors suggest that collaboration between individuals could be more effective than hierarchical organization for some tasks. By sharing, they suggest the benefit of sharing intellectual property rather than its exclusive use. By global action, the authors discuss how globalization affects collaboration, and how the new way of collaboration in turn promotes globalization.

The sharing aspect is not only about production but also about consumption. Botsman and Rogers (2011) illustrate how people are engaged in collaborative consumption ranging from sharing a car or bicycle to the reuse and recycling of goods, and they describe how people are involved in mass collaboration to share common resources. However, the distinction between consumption and production is not clear. As Botsman and Rogers (2010) illustrate, some people can earn money by lending their properties to others. The integration of production and consumption is also explained from a different perspective by Bressand (1991), which suggests that the more an economy becomes service centric, the more difficult it becomes to distinguish between producer and customer because value is created by the cooperation of both.

Tapscott and Williams (2008) discuss 'mass collaboration' as a broad term which includes various activities such as production based on the community of individuals, the user's involvement in a design, and solution seeking for a mass crowd. There is no precise definition of mass collaboration, but prior studies which cover mass collaboration generally focus on the aspect of "a large number of individuals" who are engaged in common activities. For example, Fathianathan et al. (2009) defines mass collaboration as "large numbers of people working together to perform various tasks including collaborative authoring (e.g. Wikipedia) and collaboratively developing software (e.g. Linux, Mozilla and Apache)." Qiu et al. (2010) also define collaboration as "a collaboration model based on collective actions with a large number of contributors and participants working independently but collaboratively in a single project that is modular in its nature." These definitions are particularly applicable to peer production in Tapscott and Williams (2008), who emphasize that work should be divided into small pieces so that individuals can participate. Therefore, although the original concept of mass collaboration is a broad idea which describes the collaboration of individuals en masse, prior studies gradually shift the focus to productive activity which is made by mass individuals, each of whom tackle a small part of a whole work, which is almost the same as crowdsourcing.

Crowdsourcing (Howe 2009) focuses on the participation and collaboration of individuals, but suggests a more organized form of collaboration so that each individual can participate more easily in a certain activity. Howe (2009) points out the importance of amateurs with the same level of knowledge as professionals, and opportunities to collect their knowledge and willingness to participate in an activity. From photo-sharing, civic journalism to scientific solutions, Howe shows how crowdsourcing utilizes the power of individuals who want to participate in these activities. At the same time, he suggests the importance of managing the community of participants, but keeping the unit of business small which is assigned to each participant. Whereas mass collaboration generally suggests the opportunity of participation and the collaboration of individuals, crowdsourcing suggests a more specific form of collaboration that focuses on amateur individuals and management of the community, which is designed for a certain purpose.

However, the definition of crowdsourcing is also the subject of discussion. Howe (2006) defines "crowdsourcing as representing the act of a company or institution taking a function once performed by employees and outsourcing it to an undefined (and generally large) network of people in the form of an open call." Brabham (2012) defines outsourcing as "an online, distributed problem solving and production model whereby an organization leverages the collective intelligence of an online community for a specific purpose. It is a blend of traditional, top-down, hierarchical program management and bottom-up open innovation process." However, there is a wide range of variations in the definition of crowdsourcing, so that building an integrated definition has become itself a subject of study (Estellés-Arolas and González-Ladrón-de-Guevara, 2012).

Frequently cited cases of mass collaboration and crowdsourcing are Wikipedia, Amazon Mechanical Turk, Threadless.com, iStockphoto.com, and InnoCentive.com such as is seen in Brabham (2012) and Estellés-Arolas and González-Ladrón-de-Guevara (2012). Next Stop Design (Brabham 2012) and Goldcorp challenge (Marjanovic et al., 2012) are also included as examples of crowdsourcing. Most examples in prior studies are based on North American crowdsourcing and Japan-based mass collaboration or crowdsourcing initiatives have not been well reported.

Certain prior studies deal with the risks and negative side of crowdsourcing. Frankrone (2013) shows risks for a crowd who are underpaid in unsecured employment, and the negative effect of this on traditional industry. Frankrone (2013) also points out the risk of harming a third party because of inaccuracy and low quality brought about by crowdsourcing. Related to these points, Lloret et al. (2013) conducted an experiment for quality control of crowdsourcing.

Comparing crowdsourcing and mass collaboration, the original meaning of mass collaboration, describes the general trend of the collaboration of individuals, whereas crowdsourcing describes a more specific form of collaboration characterized by the combination of top-down task design and bottom-up participation of a large number of people. However, as studies on mass collaboration gradually focused on peer production, the distinction between mass collaboration and crowdsourcing became vague.

The prior studies present several limitations. First, as seen in this section, most examples of mass collaboration in prior studies are based in North America, and Japan-based mass collaboration or crowdsourcing initiatives have not been well reported. However, a new movement, open data, is stimulating the rise of mass collaboration in Japan. Discussion of the development of crowdsourcing in Japan is one of the first goals of this book. Secondly, prior studies do not discuss how open data or generally open resources promote the collaboration of individuals. Therefore, discussion of the economic rationality of mass collaboration from an organizational economics viewpoint is the second point added in this book to the prior studies. Chapter 8 addresses this point by describing the latest developments in Japan and by providing arguments based on transaction cost economics.

2.8 Conclusion

This chapter reviewed prior studies covering the topics of analyses that will be discussed in the following chapters. A number of studies have been conducted on the impact of information technology on productivity. However, the focus of these studies has been on the direct relations between IT investment and productivity, and not an analysis on how firms utilize information technology with changes in their organizational structures. In other words, prior studies focus on the relation between input and output of the economy, but lack how IT is changing economic activities between its input and output. Additionally, most prior studies provide snapshots on the effects of various phenomena separately, but a comprehensive view has not been available.

This book, therefore, assesses the impact of information technology on the economy through the structural change in productive organizations. In particular, this book answers questions about how the development of IT affects organizational structure for production, and how these structural changes affect the Japanese economy, such as in employment and productivity. As seen in Table 2-2, this book fills in the missing points in the analysis on Asia. Prior studies do not assess the variety of effects of the international trade of information services depending on trading partners, but instead, generalizes them as one Asia, or as low-cost and high-cost countries. Unlike these studies, this book assesses the inherent variety in the outcome of trading with Asian countries.

Additionally, the literature review revealed that prior studies on each topic are in an initial stage, and there are a lot of missing points. Each of the following chapters fills in the missing points in the prior studies. These analyses also provide the building blocks for the overall implications which are discussed in the final chapter. The next part, Part II, specifically provides the foundation for an analysis on the impact of IT on organizational structures. Chapter 3 analyzes the mechanisms behind a firm's decisions on the outsourcing of information services, using transaction cost economics and service attributes, and Chapter 4 analyzes the factors that determine international production sharing in the service sector.

PART II
Information Technology and International Production Sharing

CHAPTER 3

Information Technology and the Organizational Structure of Modern Business Outsourcing

The organization of modern business has been affected by the development of information technology. Information technology, in particular, affects organizational structure through vertical disintegration and international production sharing. For example, firms outsource information services such as software development and call-center operations, and also computing services. In order to provide a fundamental analytical framework throughout this book, this chapter discusses the decisions by firms on outsourcing affected by information technology. In particular this chapter considers the outsourcing of information services as promoted by a drastic reduction of transaction costs, rather than simply by the difference in production costs. This chapter also focuses on the service attributes that affect the transaction costs of information services, and provides an analytical tool for the firm's choice of organizational structures. It also discusses the outsourcing decisions of firms by using the tool with examples of several types of outsourcing of information service.[1]

3.1 Background

Technological change has been one of the major reasons for structural change in business organizations.[2] A change in technology has

---

1 This chapter is based on Takagi and Tanaka (2013a), which has been restructured and revised for the book.
2 This chapter discusses the structure of business entities, including the unit of business operations and the relations of these units within a firm, and also the relation between firms. The change in organizational structure of firms can result in the organizational change of industrial structures or of society as a whole, but this paper primarily focuses on the organizational structure of business entities.

affected business operations, and as a consequence, new business operations have defined new organizational structures. Milgrom and Roberts (1992, p. 543) briefly summarize this change as follows: "Organizations change when their environments and the technologies they use change, and as they accumulate information and experience about what kinds of organizations work best for particular tasks."

This concept is also applicable to modern business environments. Drastic improvement of information technology (IT) has enabled firms to outsource various types of services overseas. For example, information services such as call-center operation, financial processing and software development are now outsourced overseas. These types of outsourcing are called "offshore outsourcing" of information services. Another case of outsourcing is the adaption of cloud computing. By using cloud computing, firms can use computing services that are provided by entities outside of the firm. Cloud computing saves firms from having to build and own their individual computer resources and allows firms to use and pay only the shared resources.

Cloud computing is "a model for enabling ubiquitous, convenient, on-demand network access to a shared pool of configurable computing resources" (Mell and Grance 2011). In short, cloud computing is a shared computing resource which can be used by many users. Cloud computing is categorized as public, private, and hybrid computing. Public cloud computing is shared by anonymous users globally, and private cloud computing is used by a specific organization. Hybrid combines public and private. In this chapter cloud computing refers to public cloud computing to focus on aspects of the outsourcing of computing services unless otherwise noted.

Cloud computing provides a wide range of services depending on whether it provides ready-made services or platforms on which customized services can be added. For example, SaaS (Software as a Service) provides ready-made information services for e-mail, human resource management, supply chain management, and customer relationship management. For instance, *Salesforce.com* provides services such as Customer Relationship Management (CRM).[3] On the other hand, PaaS (Platform as a Service) provides basic functions, but end-user services have to be constructed on the platform. IaaS (Infrastructure as a Service) provides the minimal set of hardware functions so that services and platforms can be added on the infrastructure. *Amazon Web Services* offers mainly platform services so that customers can create and use services on the platform.[4] In this book, cloud computing is occasionally referred to as the outsourcing of computing services.

Cloud computing services are penetrating the Japanese market. For example, firms which use cloud computing services increased from 21.6% in 2011 to 28.2% in 2012 (MIC 2013). U.S. firms utilize cloud computing about 1.7 times more than Japanese firms, but the gap is becoming closer (MIC 2013). Japanese firms are also providing cloud computing services, particularly in the Japanese market.

The outsourcing of information services and computing services is a phenomenon that affects the organization of modern business, and these services have common features. For example, both types of outsourcing utilize information technology, are outsourced globally, and have service characteristics for attributes. The outsourcing of these services affects organizational structure in the direction of vertical disintegration and international production sharing. From a macroeconomics perspective, the impact of the outsourcing could become pervasive, particularly on employment and productivity, because it can affect the role of a country in the global value chain.

Because of the potential impact on domestic employment and innovative capacity, empirical analyses on offshore outsourcing and cloud computing have been conducted, for example, in Amiti and Wei (2005, 2009); Falk and Wolfmayr (2008); Liu and Trefler (2008); Takagi and Tanaka (2012, 2014a, 2014b). However, to understand the impact of outsourcing and to discuss economic policies, analysis on the mechanisms behind the outsourcing of these

---

3 http://www.salesforce.com/products/
4 http://aws.amazon.com/

services is essential. Particularly, insight into how information technology has enabled objective information services to be divided from organizations and outsourced overseas is important in understanding the organizational structure of modern business.

An overarching framework that explains the effect of information technology on organizational structure is not available. The development of information technology has been generating new business models not only for offshore outsourcing of services and cloud computing, but also for global Internet media and commerce services. Analysis on the fundamental mechanisms of outsourcing will contribute to understanding the organizational changes associated with the adoption of information technology. Therefore, this chapter clarifies how the development of IT affects the structure of business organizations by specifically focusing on the outsourcing decisions of firms, and by providing an overarching framework for such analysis.

3.2 Theoretical Foundation

This section provides a theoretical foundation for the analysis presented in the following sections in this chapter by discussing the focal points of transaction cost economics (TCE) and service attributes.

3.2.1 Transaction cost economics

Traditionally, TCE views the boundary of firms as determined by transaction cost. Ronald Coase views tasks in an organization as conducted within the organization when it is less costly than carrying out the transactions through the market (Coase 1988). Transaction cost includes the various costs incurred to conduct transactions in the market, such as finding partners, and making and enforcing contracts[5]. Oliver E. Williamson developed Coase's theory by in-

---

5   For more detail on the contents of transaction costs, see Coase (1988) and Dahlman (1979).

troducing two important human factors behind transaction cost: opportunism and bounded rationality (Williamson 1983). Williamson showed that the market fails when these two human factors are combined with environmental conditions: bounded rationality with uncertainty, and opportunism with small-numbers exchange relations.

Under bounded rationality, the uncertainty surrounding a task provides a motivation for firms to conduct the tasks within the organization. Williamson (1983, p. 9) states, "If, in consideration of these limits, it is very costly or impossible to identify future contingencies and specify, *ex ante*, appropriate adaptations thereto, long-term contracts may be supplanted by internal organization." In order to minimize the loss caused by uncertainty of the information services, frequent and close communication is required. Therefore, uncertainty is associated with the costs for communication and traveling.

On the other hand, opportunism is caused by small-numbers exchange or "Ex Ante Small Numbers" (Williamson, 1975, p. 48). In particular, Ex Ante Small Numbers is caused because "Although a large-numbers exchange condition obtains at the outset, it is transformed during contract execution into a small-numbers exchange relation on account of (1) idiosyncratic experience associated with contract execution, and (2) failures in the human and nonhuman capital markets" (Williamson 1983 p. 29). Simply put, a first contract winner acquires specific assets such as know-how and better understanding of the contract, and this asset helps the seller win future contracts. Where a buyer cannot switch the supplier because of the specific assets that are acquired by the first contractor, a *hold-up* problem arises.

Williamson (1983) suggests that such a situation can be mitigated by conducting the activity in-house, because internal audits and hierarchical order can reduce information asymmetry and opportunism. Therefore, the outsourcing decision is also related to the prospects of opportunism by small-numbers exchange. If the outsourced activity includes a high asset specificity and the buyer faces the risk of opportunistic behavior, the buyer would conduct the activity in-house.

Williamson's (1975) solution for such opportunism and the risk of hold-up is to carry out the activity in a hierarchical organization. However, what are the exact costs for avoiding a hold-up problem if a firm outsources the project? These costs are summarized in three points. First, there is the cost for internalizing the assets which have been obtained by third-party vendors. If a vendor acquired specific assets of the client and the client did not have sufficient knowledge of the assets, the client would need to invest in claiming back the asset to avoid opportunistic behavior. The second point concerns the costs for specifying a contract. Without sufficient specification of a contract, the contents of the activity and the know-how for conducting it remain part of the vendor's knowledge. Third, there is a cost for overseeing the vendors to avoid the accumulation and hiding of specific assets of the client. These costs for internalizing assets, specifying contracts, and overseeing vendors are the major costs needed for avoiding hold-up risk in outsourcing projects, and conversely, if these costs are reduced, there is a greater chance for outsourcing the business.

TCE focuses primarily on transaction cost, which Coase (1988, p. 114) explains as follows, "In order to carry out a market transaction it is necessary to discover who it is that one wishes to deal with, to inform people that one wishes to deal and on what terms, to conduct negotiations leading up to a bargain, to draw up the contract, to undertake the inspection needed to make sure that the terms of the contract are being observed, and so on." Therefore, it is inferred that the transaction cost is externalized from the production cost which is the genuine cost for producing the goods or services. TCE does not focus on the difference in this production cost, but, in practice, production costs could be diverse across countries because they reflect the difference in factor prices. This difference in production costs has certainly promoted the outsourcing of information services. However, the difference in production cost have been obvious even before the current trend of information services outsourcing. Therefore, this study views the drastic reduction of transaction cost, rather than the reduction of production costs, as fostering the outsourcing of information services.

3.2.2 Service economy

In the marketing and management fields, services are defined to have four attributes: *intangibility, heterogeneity, simultaneous production and consumption,* and *perishability* (Zeithaml and Bitner 2003, p. 21). For example, a haircut as a service fulfills all four attributes. One cannot physically touch haircut services; the contents of the haircut differ slightly depending on the customer, because each customer's preference and property are different. Getting a haircut becomes possible under the cooperation between provider and customer, and one cannot store the haircutting services. These attributes suggest that "many services require customers to participate in creating the service product" (Lovelock and Wirtz 2004, p. 11). Because of these services attributes, outsourcing in the services sector has been limited to businesses whose specifications are easily defined, such as in electricity and water supply, finance, and construction. In other words, if the degree of service attributes changes, the tradability of the service will also change correspondingly.

Among the four attributes, *heterogeneity* and *simultaneous production and consumption* play the most important roles on transaction cost and outsourcing decisions. *Heterogeneity* represents the contents of services that are different depending on each customer. Particularly, where the contract requires a client's specific knowledge or asset, *heterogeneity* is associated with "asset specificity," which causes a small-numbers exchange and, therefore, opportunism.

Simultaneous production and consumption represent services that are produced and consumed simultaneously by interaction of the provider and customer. Also, the contents of services are not specified perfectly beforehand. Therefore, *simultaneous production and consumption* is also associated with uncertainty and bounded rationality in transaction cost economics.

The service sector is becoming more and more important to the economy, and as seen in this section, services characteristics influence the transaction costs of the services. Also, the distinction between manufacturing and services is becoming vague. Various products now include service components. On the other hand, some information services may also have a similarity to products. Cusumano (2010, p. 74) phrases this as "[...] the gradual 'servitization of products' as well as the 'productization of services'". In order to discuss the tradability of businesses including service factors, it is essential to analyze the service characteristics of the particular task.

3.2.3 Overall framework

One of the features of the present study is to combine two theories: transaction cost economics and service attributes. Considering the discussion in section 3.2, the relations between the related concepts are shown in Figure 3–1

First, heterogeneity, as one of the service attributes, requires specific assets to serve a certain client, and therefore, can cause opportunism and small-numbers exchange relations. The risk of opportunism is mitigated with the costs for avoiding the hold-up problem. As discussed in section 3.1, the costs for internalizing assets from the provider to client and specifying and overseeing contracts are the content of transaction costs. When these costs are too large, the business is conducted in a hierarchical manner. Conversely, if there is a factor which can reduce these costs, then business is more likely to be provided by third-party vendors.

Simultaneous production and consumption can cause an uncertainty of services, which is also caused by bounded rationality. In this book's context, the costs for reducing uncertainty are the communication and traveling costs between providers and customers. On the other hand, uncertainty and bounded rationality are also related to the difficulty in specifying contracts. Therefore, simultaneous production and consumption are related to the costs for avoiding the hold-up problem.

Based on these arguments, the overall framework of outsourcing

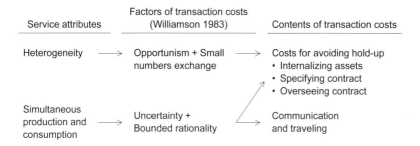

Figure 3–1. Relationships of terms

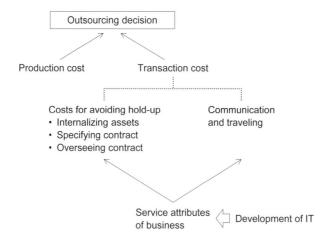

Figure 3–2. Framework of outsourcing decision

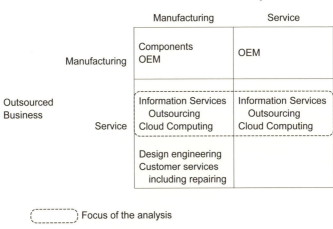

Figure 3–3. Scope of analysis

decisions is shown in Figure 3–2. This book assumes that the development of IT affects service attributes, and consequently, the change in service attributes reduces transaction costs. The reduction of these transaction costs affects the overall decisions on outsourcing.

3.2.4 Scope of analysis

When the economy is divided into manufacturing and services, the outsourcing of business processes has four variations depending on a combination of client industry and the outsourced business process. As Figure 3–3 shows, this combination of manufacturing and the service industry can outsource manufacturing or the service function. When the manufacturing sector outsources the manufacturing function, it takes the form of intermediate components or OEM (Original Equipment Manufacturer), where the manufacturing of the final products is outsourced. Recently, service firms also outsource manufacturing processes. For example, Malecki and Moriset (2008) show how Microsoft worked with Flextronics and various EMS (Electronic Manufacturing Services) for the production of the Xbox.

This chapter specifically focuses on the outsourcing of information services and computing services. These services can be outsourced both from manufacturing and service firms. Services such as sales management, human resources management and accounting are common services for most firms, and computing services are the platform for these services. Therefore, the outsourcing of information services from the manufacturing and service sector does not have a significant difference in terms of its contents and tradability. Based on this point, this book focuses on the outsourcing of information services and computing services from the manufacturing and service sector, without specifying the difference between the client industries.

3.3 Transaction Costs and Organizational Structure

Based on the arguments in the previous section about service attributes and transaction costs, this section constructs an analytical tool which operationalizes the concepts and analyzes the decisions on the organizational mode.

3.3.1 Analytical tool

Taking into account the discussion in the previous section, Figure 3–4 represents an analytical tool developed to operationalize the theories of TCE and service attributes The vertical axis shows the degree of *heterogeneity*, which also measures the costs of hold-ups such as internalizing assets and specifying and overseeing contracts. The horizontal axis shows the degree of *simultaneous production and consumption*, which also measures the costs for communication and traveling. The contents in the dashed boxes (A to E) represent the choice of a suitable organizational mode based on the combination of service attributes.

When the heterogeneity of a certain service is very high and there is a high risk of opportunism and hold-up, these services are conducted by hierarchical organization (C) because of the high costs for internalizing assets, and for specifying and overseeing contracts. On the other hand, if simultaneous production and consumption is very high, and therefore there is a high need for close communication,

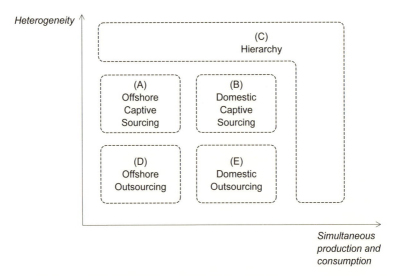

Figure 3–4. Analytical tools on organizational modes

these services are also conducted by hierarchical organization (C)⁶.

When the level of *heterogeneity* and *simultaneous production and consumption* become lower, there is a chance for outsourcing. When *heterogeneity* and the risk of opportunism is relatively high, the task is outsourced to the firms established or acquired by user firms to enjoy cost reduction while mitigating the risk of opportunism. IPA (2012) shows that among Japanese IT service firms that have experience with outsourcing software development services, 46.4% of those firms have established their own subsidiary companies, one of whose services is to provide outsourced software development. The outsourcing to the subsidiary companies is called "captive sourcing" (Gottfredson et al., 2005; Baldia, 2007). Captive sourcing combines the benefit of cost reduction and hierarchical control, while flexibility is achieved less than outsourcing to third party

---

6   There are some variations in the case of high simultaneous production and consumption. For example, firms can outsource to a provider whose workers reside in a client's location, so that providers and clients work in the same place and enable close communication. Additionally, there are cases of dispatched workers in the hierarchical organization. The choice between dispatch work or outsourcing in a client's location could also depend on the contents of the work and labor regulations.

vendors. As a result, there are choices on offshore captive sourcing (A) or domestic captive sourcing (B) when the heterogeneity is relatively higher, and offshore outsourcing (D) or domestic outsourcing (E) when the heterogeneity is lower.

On the other hand, less *simultaneous production and consumption* leads to less cost for communication, thus promoting the outsourcing of the tasks. The required costs for communication are related to the decision on domestic or international outsourcing. If the buyer and provider need close communication and coordination on the activity, it is less easy to outsource the project overseas because of the difference of language, cultural norms, and business customs. Conversely, if the required proximity becomes less important, it becomes easier to outsource the project overseas. As a result, the level of *simultaneous production and consumption* defines the choice between domestic (B, E) or offshore (A, D) outsourcings[7].

The present study focuses on service attributes and transaction costs as factors on outsourcing decisions. However, there is a growing concern with information security regarding outsourcing projects, such as the risk of leakage of confidential information and personal data. In prior studies, Gonzalez et al. (2008) list security problems as one of the risks of information systems outsourcing. They point out the importance of keeping confidentiality when providers are serving several competitors. Because the development of information technology has made it easier for information to be copied and transferred globally, the risk of security is higher when information protection has to be enforced across different organizations in outsourcing projects. The costs for security consideration and the associated risks are also one of the transaction costs in the choice of organizational structures.

---

7 This book focuses on the effect of IT, but there is also another factor that reduces uncertainty. For example, improvement of contract terms also affects the tradability of services. Blair et al. (2011) identified several important features to reduce uncertainty such as a "Master Agreement" plus "Statement of Work" structure, identifying a small number of key personnel as decision-makers, invoking or developing standardized metrics, codification of processes, and periodic evaluation of performance against standards. These contractual improvements also reduce uncertainty in outsourcing projects.

3.4 Application of the Analytical Tool

This section experimentally applies the analytical tool discussed in section 4 and analyzes the choice of firms on outsourcing. It discusses the effect of information technology on the firm's decisions on organizational structure by considering several cases: software development, call-center operation, and cloud computing. The analysis is mainly based on prior studies on the history of related technology and business.

3.4.1 Software development

In terms of software development, *heterogeneity* has been significant particularly for customized software projects, therefore, defining the specifications of the projects has been important (Cataldo and Herbsleb 2013; Palacio et al. 2011; Gopal et al. 2011). Even in outsourcing projects, specification is still important for software development, and mediation by bridge-SE (the vendor's system engineer who resides in a clients' location) is adopted in outsourcing projects (Umezawa 2007). In this sense, *heterogeneity* has not changed. Therefore, the choice between captive or non-captive sourcing depends on the original level of the heterogeneity of each project.

Then again, required *simultaneous production and consumption* and associated costs for communication have been reduced with the development of information technology such as TV conferencing and development management tools. For example, Palacio et al. (2011) provide a comprehensive survey on distributed software development (DSD). They propose the use of instant messaging (IM) and collaborative working spheres (CWS) to support communication, and the use of personal activity management (PAM) to help project management. In general, the introduction of technologies to support communication, to manage source code and product, and to help project management are important to enable the offshore outsourcing of software development. Because of the reduction of *simultaneous production and consumption*, firms are more likely to out-

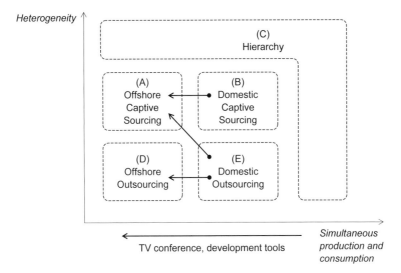

Figure 3–5. Organizational structure of software development

source the development process.

In a Japanese context, development of customized software is often outsourced from user firms to IT vendors, and from IT vendors to third-party software companies (IPA 2011). This "multi-layer outsourcing" used to be conducted domestically, but outsourcing overseas has grown since the early 2000s (IPA 2010). IPA (2011) points out that under a multi-layer outsourcing industrial structure, offshore outsourcing of software development has raised the downward pressure of prices for small- and medium-sized IT firms.

Based on this domestic background in Japan, software development has been conducted through domestic captive sourcing (B) or domestic outsourcing (E) as in Figure 3–5, depending on the heterogeneity of the software. When firms outsource the development process overseas, they have a choice to take offshore captive sourcing (A) or offshore outsourcing (D). In order to reduce the risk of opportunism in an offshore outsourcing project, offshore captive outsourcing (A) has been also one of the options. Usually captive sourcing is more costly then outsourcing, but the difference of prices across countries may offset the cost associated with establishing subsidiary companies abroad.

The analysis on the example on the role of development tools in the outsourcing decision needs in-depth case studies. However, there are several cases on offshore outsourcing of software development. Saisho (2010) introduces the case where Hitachi Software Engineering (now Hitachi Solutions) established an offshore development center in Hanoi, Vietnam, in 2005, by ensuring a system development team in FPT software, a Vietnamese software company. This case seems to combine the benefits of offshore captive sourcing (A) and offshore outsourcing (D). Saisho (2010) also raises the case of CSC, a U.S. based company, which acquired a Vietnamese software company, FCG, to provide software development and maintenance services. This is a case of the offshore captive sourcing (A), developed by M&A.

3.4.2 Call-center operation

In terms of call-center operation, *simultaneous production and consumption* has also been reduced by the introduction of technology. Call-center operators have to share customers' information with other business departments to respond to various customers' demands. However, the introduction of CRM (Customer Relationship Management) systems based on broadband network have drastically reduced communication costs between call-centers in distant locations and in other departments.

CRM systems are computer systems designed typically to support call-center operators in recording and managing interactions with customers, but there are various functions in CRM systems. Torggler (2009) classifies CRM systems by functions and stages of business, and shows that CRM systems support various activities such as recording customer data, marketing support, complaint management, and data analysis for marketing, sales, and services. CRM systems, therefore, provide various functions for managing data on customers and sales, but this data is used by various organizations such as marketing, sales, and customer support.

With the introduction of CRM, the record on customer support activity is simultaneously shared by business headquarters and

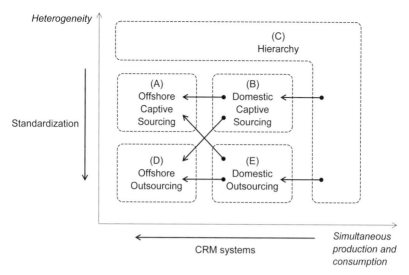

Figure 3–6. Organizational structure of call-center operation

call-centers, and a summary of information can be reported periodically from call-center operations. Thus, the development of CRM systems has reduced *simultaneous production and consumption* and associated communication costs between call centers and other departments.

The organizational structure for call-center operations is shown in Figure 3–6. Traditionally, call-center operations have been conducted within organizations through a hierarchy (C). Generally, the development of IT such as in CRM systems has reduced the *simultaneous production and consumption* attributes. On the other hand, there is a possibility that penetration of CRM may promote the standardization of customer management business and therefore reduce *heterogeneity*. However, the information on each customer is different and even confidential for each firm. Therefore, the choice between captive or non-captive sourcing depends on the original level of heterogeneity in each firm.

Moshi Moshi Hotline, a Japan-based company that provides call-center services for customers, owns subsidiary companies in Vietnam and China, for providing call-center services (Nikkei sangyo shinbun 2014). This company provides various back office services including customer relations from an office in Dalian, China, and standardization is one of the service for customers.[8] The establishment of offshore sites of the company in China and Vietnam exemplifies the transition from domestic outsourcing (E) to offshore outsourcing (D).

3.4.3 Cloud computing

Computing services in general used to be provided within an organization because of the necessity of customization for each organization. However, along with the convergence of optimal business processes, provision of standardized services for a large volume of customers in the form of cloud computing has become more economical.

For example, Bills (2014) shows that the way to realize the value of cloud computing is through standardization and simplification, and raises several examples in which firms benefit from standardization of business processes in the course of adopting cloud computing. McNeill et al. (2011) provide the result of a survey that shows access to standardized business processes is the motivation for outsourcing for 80% of user firms. This standardization reduces the heterogeneity of computing services.[9]

On the other hand, *virtualization*,[10] a technological innovation for cloud computing, has enabled many firms to share the same computing resources. Additionally, penetration of broadband networks such as fiber-optics has also allowed responsive functionality in distant locations. Thus, virtualization and an improved network infrastructure have reduced the required proximity between computing services and user firms.

---

8   http://www.moshimoshi.co.jp/offshore/dalian.html. Accessed August 25, 2014.
9   Baldwin and Clark (1997, 2000) introduced the concept of modularity to deal with complex systems. Modularity consists of sub elements: abstraction of functions, information hiding within each module, and interface to define the interaction between modules. Public cloud computing is analogous to the modularity of computing services in terms of information hiding and specification of interface. This modularization can also reduce the heterogeneity of computing services.
10 Virtualization is a technological element which enables users to utilize the shared computing resource as if the resource is used only by the user.

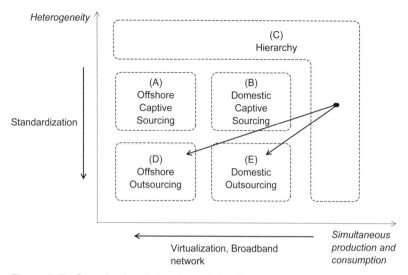

Figure 3-7. Organizational structure of cloud computing

The organizational structure of cloud computing is shown in Figure 3–7. In terms of public cloud computing[11], the choice for firms is whether to use domestic or international cloud services (C to D or E). The choice between them depends on the requirements for close communication. If the service requires close communication between providers and clients, the firm will choose domestic outsourcing. Other factors such as regulation on personal information protection, or business contingency would also affect the decision on using domestic or international cloud computing.

One example of international cloud computing is Google Apps, which provides various tools such as email, video conferencing, scheduling, and word-processing.[12] Google Apps is used by Japanese firms such as ANA, Beams, and Misawa Homes.[13] The exact location of the data centers of the service is not available, but generally, the location of the data centers in cloud computing services is not limited in Japan.

---

11 On the difference of public, private, and hybrid cloud computing, see section 1.
12 http://www.google.com/intx/ja/enterprise/apps/business/about/. Accessed August 28, 2014
13 http://www.google.com/intx/ja/enterprise/apps/business/case-studies/. Accessed August 28, 2014

Table 3–1. Comparison of the three cases on transaction costs

Service attributes	Heterogeneity	Simultaneous production and consumption
Factors to lower the attributes	Standardization	Communication networks and tools
Software development	High	High
Call-center operation (BPO: Business process outsourcing)	Middle	Middle
Cloud computing	Low	Low

3.5 A Comparison of the Three Cases

Previous sections analyzed the change in service attributes and transaction cost in each business case: software development, call-center operation, and cloud computing. But how are these three cases different in terms of the absolute level of transaction costs? There is no effective way to measure the transaction costs across different cases, but from analyses in previous sections, the absolute level of heterogeneity and simultaneous production and consumption is compared as seen in Table 3–2.

As discussed previously, *heterogeneity* of software development is traditionally high because of the required coordination for customization. The level of *simultaneous production and consumption* is also high, but it can be reduced by the introduction of communication tools.

On the other hand, cloud computing is the result of the standardization of business processes, which reduces *heterogeneity*. It is also the result of virtualization and broadband networks, which reduce the requirement for *simultaneous production and consumption*. In a sense, cloud computing is the result of the effort to reduce transaction cost for information services; therefore, the absolute levels of both of service attributes are low.

Call-center operation, or in general, business process outsourcing, falls somewhere between software development and cloud computing. Compared to software development, call-center operation could be more standardized, because customization is less frequent or comprehensive. However, its service attributes are higher than cloud computing, because it is not fully computerized and needs to be conducted manually by human staff.

Therefore, in comparing the three cases, transaction cost is highest in software development, medium for business process outsourcing, and lowest for cloud computing. This comparison is referred to in the following chapters together with the results of the analyses in each chapter.

3.6 Conclusions

This chapter has analyzed the mechanisms behind a firm's decision to use outsourcing of information services, by considering transaction cost economics and service attributes. This chapter therefore has provided a framework and analytical tool to operationalize the theory of TCE to better understand a firm's choice on organizational structure. Experimental application of the tool on examples shows that the tool helps a firm's understanding of the influence of IT on service attributes and transaction cost, and how service attributes and transaction cost affect the firm's choice of organizational structure. Compared to prior studies, this book discusses IT as an enabler of outsourcing, and analyzes the effect of IT on a firm's decision of its organizational structure.

More specifically, this chapter has shown that how the development of IT has affected the structure of business organizations through decisions on outsourcing. In particular, the analysis showed that the change in service attributes such as in *heterogeneity* and *simultaneous production and consumption* play important roles for outsourcing decisions. This chapter also discussed how standardization is an important factor affecting *heterogeneity*, and how communication networks and tools are important factors for *simultaneous production and consumption*. Practically, promotion of the outsourcing of information services is determined by standardization and communication networks and tools.

The service sector, in general, in its relation to trade, has become more standardized, and this standardization is related to the adoption of information technology. In terms of CRM or cloud computing, standardization evolves as major suppliers provide services to more customers, which results in *de facto* standards. Standardization is also a subject of economic policy. In the software development field, development processes, quality management, and IT skills have been discussed in various standardization endeavors both at the national and international level. These discussions result in various *de jure* standards such as those adopted by the International Organization for Standardization. From an economic policy point of view, it is important to understand what services can be standardized and are likely to be outsourced in order to form effective industry and employment policy.

This chapter sheds light on the changes in transaction cost as determinants on the outsourcing of services, but as the experimental application shows, there are many other factors that could also affect outsourcing decisions, such as regulations on data protection, information security, the core competency of firms, and the effect on knowledge creation and spillover, for example. Understanding how these factors also affect these aspects and integrating these aspects into transaction cost analysis is a subject for future work.

To achieve the goal of this book, which is the assessment of the impact of IT on the economy through organizational changes, this chapter provided a fundamental view on the relationship between IT and organizational structure. In particularly, this chapter discussed how IT affects organizational structures in terms of several modes of organizational structure, and the difference of tradability of several information services, such as software development, call-center operation, and cloud computing. The next chapter discusses the reasoning behind the choices of the location of outsourcing and therefore, the location of foreign direct investment in service sector, focusing on cultural characteristics as key determinants.

CHAPTER 4
Foreign Direct Investment in the Service Sector and National Culture

4.1 Introduction

The service sector is becoming more important in the modern economy. It has more presence not only as a major composition in national economy, but also as a subject for international trade and foreign direct investments. As a result, the share of service sectors in the national products of most countries ranged from 72% to 52% and the FDI inflow in the sectors accounted for about two-thirds of total FDI inflow over 2001–2002 (UNCTAD 2004, pp. 97–98). Structural changes from the manufacturing sectors to the service sectors are partly due to deregulation in various industries such as telecommunications, finance, and other infrastructure services in most developing countries. The other factor is the rise of services using new technologies, such as IT-services and IT-enabled services (ITES). Thus, service sectors are shifting from national to transnational, non-tradable to tradable. In the context of this book, it is important to consider that IT is becoming more and more a provided service, and as such is affected by the characteristics of services.[1]

The success of the transnationalization of the service sectors, whether it is for establishing production capacity or searching new markets, depends on how the service sectors are accepted in a foreign society. The service sector is generally regarded as having four characteristics: *intangibility, heterogeneity, simultaneous production and consumption*, and *perishability* (Zeithaml and Bitner 2003, p. 21). *Simultaneous production and consumption* represents production and

---

[1] This chapter is based on Takagi, S., Tanaka, H. and Sonoda, S. (2011).

consumption taking place at the same time. This simultaneity is related to the idea that "many services require customers to participate in creating the service product" (Lovelock and Wirtz 2004, p. 11). These characteristics mean that the value of services depends on the interaction between providers and customers. Therefore, the value of most services depends on communications and the way they are delivered, which in turn relates to national culture.[2] For this reason, it is important to assess how national culture accepts services of foreign MNCs. In this chapter, national culture is analyzed as a key determinant for FDI inflow, with a comparison of different impacts in both service and non-service sectors.[3]

4.2 The AsiaBarometer

This research uses variables of the AsiaBarometer, as proxy variables of national culture. The AsiaBarometer is a comprehensive survey on national culture in Asian economies, covering East Asia to Southeast Asia, South Asia, and Middle Asia. It is organized by three Japanese universities: Chuo University, the University of Tokyo, and Waseda University.[4]

The AsiaBarometer focuses on the "daily lives of ordinary people and their relationships to family, neighborhood, workplace, social and political institutions and the marketplace" and employs a face-to-face questionnaire.[5] The survey has been conducted every year in different countries since 2003, and as of December, 2009, included 32 countries. The economies which are included in this analysis are listed in Appendix 4–A. Whereas Hofstede's data is based on a survey on business people in various countries (Hofstede 1983), the

---

2 This study assumes that cultural characteristics are represented by several key indicators following Hofstede (2001). However, this study also derives original indicators using the AsiaBarometer combinations as variables to represent national culture.
3 For more detail of multinational corporations in the service sector from the perspective of the study of management, see Campbell and Verbeke (1994), Lovelock and Yip (1996), etc.
4 https://www.asiabarometer.org/en/index. (Accessed on July 10, 2011)
5 https://www.asiabarometer.org/en/profile. (Accessed on July 10, 2011)

AsiaBarometer represents the values of diverse citizens, from urban to rural areas so that the AsiaBarometer is more suitable to assess the acceptance of services from foreign MNCs for consumers.

This research uses the AsiaBarometer data from 2004 to 2007 and economic data from 2000 to 2002. This disparity of the period is due to the limitation of availability of sector-divided FDI data. To assess the consistency of cultural characteristic in the Asia-Barometer, differences in cultural variables across economies and over years are compared. In order to assess consistency, eight to ten economies,[6] which answered the survey twice among a total of 27 economies, are used because the country coverage of the Asia-Barometer is different over the years.

As Williamson (1983) pointed out, the social embeddedness level of institutions changes very slowly, so that cultural variables may be thought of as relatively stable. For these reasons, the AsiaBarometer from 2004 to 2007 with FDI statistics from 2000 to 2002 are used in this book.

4.3 Methodology

4.3.1 Two models

Two different estimation models are employed in this analysis. First, four cultural variables of the AsiaBarometer that influence FDI are accessed in model 1. However, variables which are not used in model 1 still have the possibility to characterize national culture. Therefore, second, cultural variables are compounded to abstract cultural characteristics. The second model employs factor analysis to abstract cultural characteristics from related variables, and uses factors from regression analysis.

---

6 The number of economies depends on the variables in the survey.

4.3.2 Model 1

The first model is as follows:

$$Y = \alpha + \beta_1(FDIlagged) + \beta_2(GDP) + \beta_3(TOC) + \beta_4(AFM) \\ + \beta_5(NAT) + \beta_6(ENG) + e \qquad (4\text{--}1)$$

where Y represents three types of FDI inflow as dependent variables: total FDI inflow, service FDI inflow, and non-service FDI inflow, each divided by GDP. FDI data is the average of 2000 to 2002, and GDP is also the average of the corresponding period.

FDI lagged is used to control the agglomeration effect of FDI. FDI is attracted to locations in which other foreign MNCs have already invested. As Katsaitis and Doulos (2009) used lagged FDI to include the agglomeration effect, the log of average FDI in the precedent period (1997–1999) is used in this analysis. GDP is included in this model as the size of the market. Bevan and Estrin (2004) also used GDP to include market size. Dependent variables are already divided by GDP to represent the intensity of FDI inflow. However, the intensity of FDI may still be influenced by the market size. Therefore, GDP is included in the model as a proxy to better access the potential market. In this model, the log of average GDP in the corresponding period (2000–2002) is used.

Four other variables are based on the questions in the Asia-Barometer. TOC stands for Technology Oriented Culture, and TOC is based on questions as to whether people prefer technological development or prefer respect for traditional authority. AFM stands for Acceptance of Foreign Multinational Corporations. AFM is based on the question as to whether people trust multinational corporations operating in their country. POC stands for Proud of Own Country, and is based on the question as to the extent of being proud of one's own country first. ENG is fluency of English, based on the answers in the survey. OLS analysis is used to estimate the coefficients.

The summary of the statistics in model 1 is shown in Table 4–1. There is no outlier with the standard so that values are within the means plus/minus four standard deviations. For both models 1 and

Table 4–1 Summary of statistics in variables in model 1

	N	Min	Max	Mean	SD
Total FDI/GDP	18	0.001	0.191	0.047	0.055
Service FDI/GDP	16	−0.002	0.184	0.027	0.047
Non-service FDI/GDP	16	0.003	0.087	0.025	0.026
Log of FDI lagged	18	2.576	10.685	6.916	2.169
Log of GDP	18	0.163	7.190	3.633	1.955
TOC	18	0.045	1.188	0.476	0.312
AFM	18	2.079	3.515	2.568	0.324
POC	18	2.809	3.954	3.603	0.342
ENG	18	1.249	3.330	1.951	0.539

18 cases are used in the analysis of Total FDI, and 16 cases are used in the analysis for service FDI and non-service FDI due to the limitations of the FDI statistics.

2, the VIFs of cultural variables range from 1.049 to 3.016. The VIFs of the Log of FDI lagged and the Log of GDP range from 3.482 to 8.443. All correlations of variables are shown in Table 4–4.

4.3.3 Model 2

Factor analysis on the AsiaBarometer variables was conducted to abstract cultural characteristics more comprehensively. Principal Axis Factoring was conducted with promax rotation for seven variables. Table 4–2 shows the result of the rotation with a factor analysis of seven variables.

Conservativeness mostly represents cultures which respect keeping a national order. Internationalism represents cultures which have fluency in English and a rich foreign contact experience. Nationalism represents cultures that have a strong degree of pride in their own country. The means of the three factors for each economy were calculated and used as the economies' cultural variables in the regression analysis. The mean score for each economy is shown in Appendix 4–B. The estimation model with the factor analysis is as follows:

Table 4–2 Promax rotation of 3 factors of the 7 variables in the Asia-Barometer

Variable	Factors			Communalities after the analysis
	Conservativeness	Internationalism	Nationalism	
Belongingness to a transnational group	−.118	.084	.278	.075
Proud of Own Country	.058	−.026	.568	.348
English Fluency	−.034	.610	.131	.382
Acceptance of foreign MNCs	.047	.110	.087	.024
Foreign Contact Experience	.022	.677	−.089	.470
Technology-Oriented Culture	.093	−.056	−.014	.011
Importance of keeping national order	.419	.043	−.042	.170

N=13043, Shaded areas represent a contribution more than .20

Table 4–3 Summary of statistics in independent variables in model 2

	N	Min	Max	Mean	SD
Total FDI/GDP	16	0.001	0.191	0.045	0.054
Service FDI/GDP	14	−0.002	0.184	0.028	0.050
Non-service FDI/GDP	14	0.003	0.073	0.022	0.021
Log of FDI lagged	16	2.576	10.685	6.975	2.301
Log of GDP	16	0.163	7.190	3.709	2.016
Conservativeness	16	−0.497	0.349	0.005	0.215
Internationalism	16	−0.466	1.419	0.037	0.458
Nationalism	16	−0.680	0.394	0.005	0.334

Other variables are the same as in model 1. 16 cases are used in the analysis of total FDI, and 14 cases are used in the analysis for service FDI and non-service FDI due to the limitations of the FDI statistics.

Table 4-4 Correlations of variables

	Total FDI/GDP	Service FDI/GDP	Non-service FDI/GDP	Log of FDI lagged	Log of GDP	TOC	AFM	POC	ENG	Conservativeness	Internationalism	Nationalism
Total FDI/GDP	1											
Service FDI/GDP	.888***	1										
Non-service FDI/GDP	.570**	.129	1									
Log of FDI lagged	.433*	.415	.155	1								
Log of GDP	.055	.169	-.153	.844***	1							
TOC	-.202	-.249	-.121	.210	.183	1						
AFM	.218	-.040	.517**	.256	.038	-.004	1					
POC	-.427*	-.542**	.126	-.379	-.327	.338	.211	1				
ENG	.302	.338	.319	.175	.163	-.302	.410*	.175	1			
Conservativeness	-.443*	-.551**	.205	-.259	-.265					1		
Internationalism	.335	.391	.258	.059	.026					.171	1	
Nationalism	-.532**	-.543**	-.081	-.244	-.162					.707***	.065	1

Pearson correlations. ***, **, * denote the 1%, 5%, and 10% level of significance

$$Y = \alpha + \beta_1(FDIlagged) + \beta_2(GDP) + \beta_3(Conservativeness)$$
$$+ \beta_4(Internationalism) + \beta_5(Nationalism) + e \qquad (4-2)$$

where FDI lagged and GDP are the same as those employed in estimation model 1. Conservativeness, Internationalism, and Nationalism are elements obtained by the factor analysis. OLS analysis is used to estimate coefficients. The summary of statistics of model 2 is shown in Table 4–3. It is confirmed that there is no outlier with the standard so that all values are within the means plus/minus four standard deviations. Correlations of the variables are shown in Table 4–4.

4.4 Results

4.4.1 Model 1

Table 4–5 shows the results of model 1. High POC, which represents the extent of being proud of one's own country, has a negative effect for service FDI, whereas it has no significant effect on non-service FDI or total FDI. English fluency in the host economy has a positive effect on the total FDI inflow, whereas it is not statistically significant for both service FDI and non-service FDI. However, the estimated beta coefficients of English fluency are positive for service FDI and negative for non-service FDI. Therefore, the positive effect of English fluency for total FDI might be due possibly to the positive effect for service FDI.

4.4.2 Model 2

Table 4–6 shows the results of model 2. Conservativeness, which represents mostly keeping the national order, has a negative effect for service FDI inflow, whereas it has no significant effect for non-service FDI. Internationalism, which represents English fluency and foreign contact experience, is a positive determinant of total FDI inflow. However, it has no significant effect on sector-divided FDI.

Table 4–5 Variable estimation of model 1

Dependent Variable	Total FDI/GDP		Service FDI/GDP		Non-Service FDI/GDP	
Model variation	(1)	(2)	(1)	(2)	(1)	(2)
ln FDIlagged	.034***(.008)	.032***(.009)	.028**(.011)	.025*(.012)	.017**(.006)	.015(.008)
Log of GDP	-.030***(.009)	-.034***(.009)	-.021*(.012)	-.027**(.011)	-.018**(.006)	-.014*(.008)
TOC		.000(.038)		.015(.038)		-.016(.027)
AFM		-.025(.033)		-.046(.032)		.019(.023)
POC		-.060(.037)		-.075*(.038)		.015(.027)
ENG		.041*(.021)		.036(.022)		-.004(.016)
Constant	-.079**(.036)	.148(.129)	-.095*(.048)	.256*(.136)	-.032(.026)	-.119(.098)
Adjusted R^2	.460	.591	.243	.487	.307	.152

N=18,16,16 for TotalFDI/GDP, ServiceFDI/GDP, Non-Service FDI/GDP respectively. Standard errors in parentheses. ***, **, * denote the 1%, 5%, and 10% level of significance

Table 4-6 Variable estimation of model 2

Dependent Variable	Total FDI/GDP		Service FDI/GDP		Non-Service FDI/GDP	
Model	(1)	(2)	(1)	(2)	(1)	(2)
ln FDIlagged	.032***(.010)	.028(.008)	.031**(.014)	.034(.011)	.013*(.006)	.010(.008)
Log of GDP	-.027**(.011)	-.026(.009)	-.025(.015)	-.032(.011)	-.012*(.007)	-.009(.008)
Conservativeness		-.081(.058)		-.163**(.063)		.037(.047)
Internationalism		.043**(.019)		.022(.020)		.004(.014)
Nationalism		-.033(.036)		.011(.042)		-.021(.031)
Constant	-.076*(.039)	-.051(.031)	-.105*(.056)	-.102(.046)	-.026(.025)	-.013(.034)
Adjusted R^2	.392	.645	.230	.645	.158	-.069

N=16,14,14 for TotalFDI/GDP, ServiceFDI/GDP, Non-Service FDI/GDP respectively. Standard errors in parentheses.
***,**,* denote the 1%, 5%, and 10% level of significance

4.5 Discussion

In model 1, high POC had a negative effect on service FDI and English fluency had a positive effect on total FDI. A possible explanation is that strong POC tends to impede adaptation of foreign services which includes the cultural context of investing countries. Contrary to expectations, acceptance of foreign MNCs had no significant effect for FDI in any sectors. A possible explanation is that the response in the questionnaire for AFM includes the impression on existing MNCs in the economy and expectations on MNCs, which are not yet active in the economy. This vagueness on the responses may have influenced the estimation.

In model 2, conservativeness had a negative effect on service FDI. This effect is not found in the non-service sector. Internationalism had a significant positive effect in accepting total FDI. However, it had no specific effect on sector-divided FDI inflow.

In general, the non-service sector has a smaller R^2; therefore it can be inferred that the non-service sector is little affected by cultural variables. Non-service FDI may be more determined by other variables, such as labor cost, infrastructure, and market growth, etc. From an economic policy point of view, when a country tries to promote its service sector by FDI, culture is important in influencing the acceptance of foreign services. In particular, a strong pride of one's own country and conservativeness might stimulate FDI inflow in the service sector. Conversely, if a country tries to promote an export in the service sector, it is important to assess the national culture in the market to accept its services.[7]

4.6 Conclusion

This chapter provided statistical evidence to support the hypothesis that FDI in the service sector is influenced by cultural characteris-

---

[7] There is the possibility that the entry mode can alter the degree of cultural effect. For example, joint ventures with local companies might make the services more acceptable for consumers because the services are provided by local organizations.

tics in a host country. As seen in previous sections, national culture influences service FDI in various ways, compared to the non-service sector.

However, this analysis has several limitations. Due to data availability, the number of cases is relatively small. A more concrete estimation would be possible with a more comprehensive dataset, such as a time series of the AsiaBarometer, and updated sector-specific FDI statistics. Also, there is the possibility that cultural characteristics may be embedded in regulation on FDI. Research on the relationships between culture and regulation, and the effects of regulation on FDI are subjects for future study. Because the service sectors consist of diverse business sectors, analysis on each business sector would be beneficial in finding the effects of national culture and the nature of each service sector. This chapter assessed the effects on the service sector in general, instead of specifically on the information services sector due to data availability. Information services share common characteristics of services, but specific analysis on information services sector is desirable in clarifying the unique characteristics of information services and deriving its implications on the industry. More specific analysis is also a future challenge.

In order to achieve the goal of this book which is the assessment of the impact of IT on the economy through organizational changes, Part II provided a fundamental view on the relationship between IT and organizational structure. In particular, Chapter 3 discussed how IT affects organizational structures in terms of several modes of organizational structure, and the difference of tradability of several information services, such as software development, call-center operation, and cloud computing. On the other hand, Chapter 4 discussed how the location of foreign direct investment is determined, focusing on the cultural characteristics as a key determinant. Based on the discussion on the organizational structure in Part II, the chapters in Part III discuss the specific form of outsourcing and organizational changes and assess the effects on macroeconomic variables. The implications of the following analyses are discussed in each chapter, combined with insights on tradability and organizational structure which are provided in this chapter.

Appendix 4-A. Economies in the AsiaBarometer and survey year

Economy	2004	2005	2006	2007
Afghanistan		○		
Bangladesh		◎		
Bhutan		○		
Brunei	◎			
Cambodia	□			◎
China, Mainland	□		◎	
Hong Kong			◎	
India		◎*		
Indonesia	□			○
Japan	□		□	
Kazakhstan		◎		
Korea, Republic of	□		□	
Kyrgyzstan		◎		
Laos	□			○
Malaysia	□			◎
Maldives		○		
Mongolia		◎		
Myanmar	□			○
Nepal		◎*		
Pakistan		◎		
Philippines	□			◎
Singapore	□		◎	
Sri Lanka		◎		
Taiwan			◎	
Tajikistan		○		
Thailand	□			◎
Turkmenistan		○		
Uzbekistan		○		
Vietnam	□		◎	

◎ Used in the analysis, ○ Not used due to data availability, □ Used to analyze data consistency
* Used only for the analysis of total FDI

Appendix 4-B. Cultural variables of countries in the AsiaBarometer

Economy/Region	TOC	AFM	POC	ENG	Conservativeness	Internationalism	Nationalism
Bangladesh	0.83	2.65	3.84	1.86	0.183	−0.092	0.205
Brunei Darussalam	0.41	3.51	3.84	2.54	–	–	–
Cambodia	0.88	2.63	3.81	1.53	0.069	0.045	0.173
China, Mainland	0.78	2.55	3.36	1.47	0.000	−0.466	−0.232
Hong Kong	0.26	2.36	2.81	2.03	−0.497	0.133	−0.680
India	0.44	2.66	3.9	2.45	−0.001	0.019	0.383
Kazakhstan	0.32	2.33	3.39	1.25	−0.059	−0.376	−0.384
Kyrgyz Republic	0.33	2.58	3.42	1.28	0.108	−0.313	−0.196
Malaysia	0.16	2.88	3.49	2.02	−0.003	0.175	0.006
Mongolia	0.19	2.08	3.8	1.46	−0.154	−0.320	0.113
Nepal	0.25	2.35	3.75	2.4	0.248	0.576	0.049
Pakistan	0.64	2.3	3.72	1.64	–	–	–
Philippines	0.05	2.81	3.85	2.28	−0.026	0.199	0.302
Singapore	0.27	2.78	3.44	3.33	0.123	1.419	−0.060
Sri Lanka	0.34	2.19	3.75	2.42	0.005	0.163	0.226
Taiwan	0.36	2.4	2.84	1.58	−0.392	−0.154	−0.567
Thailand	1.19	2.42	3.95	1.83	0.133	−0.332	0.394
Vietnam	0.87	2.73	3.89	1.76	0.349	−0.084	0.345

PART III
Information Technology and
the Japanese Economy

CHAPTER 5
Offshore Outsourcing of Information Services and Employment

Based on the organizational view presented in Part II, this discussion spotlights the impact of organizational change on the economy. This chapter focuses on the "past" stage, by focusing on the offshore outsourcing of information services overseas by empirically assessing the impact of offshore outsourcing on Japanese employment from 2002 to 2006, and specifying the partner countries to which the services are outsourced. Additionally, partner countries are related to the objective business processes which are outsourced from Japan. The results show that information services outsourcing affects employment in the manufacturing sector in Japan, but the impact is different depending on trading partners. In particular, the outsourcing to OECD countries reduces manufacturing employment in Japan. On the other hand, the outsourcing to China increases such manufacturing, and outsourcing to India reduces manufacturing employment in Japan. The different impact across trading partners is discussed related to the object of trade, such as software development, cloud computing, and business process outsourcing.[1]

5.1 Introduction

Since the turn of the new millennium, pervasive use of ICT has changed the ways of business in almost all industries. Since the middle of 2000s especially, ICT has played a role in rebuilding organizational networks by connecting value chains and providing

---
[1] This chapter is based on Takagi and Tanaka (2011) and Takagi and Tanaka (2014a), which are restructured and revised for this book.

communication networks with drastically lower costs. This change has two important aspects. First, the use of ICT has lowered the cost to build production networks across distant locations and across borders. Second, ICT has made certain types of services tradable, which used to be non-tradable and had to be produced at the same location of consumption.

For example, software development, software-related research and development (R&D), and system operations, can be performed in distant locations as long as they are connected to communication networks. In addition, information services such as call-center operations, data entry, and financial processing can now also be performed in distant locations in the form of BPO (Business Process Outsourcing). Recently, computing resources with packaged services have also been outsourced in the form of cloud computing. As a result, the value chain of many types of services has been fragmented and transferred across borders. These services together are called "information services" unless otherwise noted. The outsourcing of services to providers overseas is called "offshoring" or "offshore outsourcing."

The fragmentation of the production network of information services has been led by U.S. firms, which have outsourced their services to countries such as India, Ireland, and Israel. Those new types of trade are spreading to East Asia, typically in outsourcing from Japan to China and ASEAN countries. According to IPA (2011), Japanese IT-service firms are outsourcing their software development processes mostly to China, India, the Philippines, and Vietnam in Asian developing countries.[2]

As in the U.S., the trend of offshore outsourcing has raised concerns about its effect on employment, labor structure and growth strategy in Japan. According to IPA (2011), although the share of the outsourcing of software development services from Japan is under 1% of the overall market, offshoring is affecting the industry in ways such as the downward pressure of unit cost and the

---

2 IPA (2011), p. 109

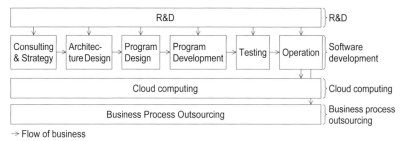

Figure 5–1. Components of information services

need for Japanese firms to shift to more upstream processes.[3]

However, employment involved in information services includes diverse knowledge and skills. Some business processes, R&D, for example, require high-level knowledge and skills, and countries need to invest in higher education for the long term to raise the capacity of R&D. On the other hand, testing and operations and system management are generally considered as more labor-intensive processes. Therefore, it is important to identify which business processes are outsourced, in order to assess the impact on labor composition and the industrial structure of developed countries.

Figure 5–1 shows the components of information services. Software development follows the business process flow from consulting and strategy, design, and development to the start of operations. R&D affects all of these processes by improving the business process and also by providing new software components and ideas. Business process outsourcing such as the outsourcing of call-center operations and financial processing is one of the results of the development of software and information systems. Cloud computing services are also enabled by the utilization of cutting-edge technology and are closely related to R&D.

In order to examine the differences in the effects of offshore outsourcing on the economy across trading partners, the amount of offshore outsourcing and its effects are analyzed in the following sections based on the available data. There is no clear way to identify which business processes are outsourced to which countries, but

---

3 IPA (2011), p. 139

IPA (2011) provides the result of a survey on the processes which are outsourced from Japan to several countries. It shows that China, India, Vietnam and the Philippines provide services from program design to testing, but the share of architecture design and more comprehensive testing is increasing. The survey also reports that India is increasing in more high-skilled processes such as R&D.

The outsourcing of information services to China also has a unique advantage. The Nikkei Sangyo shinbun (2014) reports that more than 10,000 Chinese workers process Japanese manuscripts based on the knowledge of Chinese characters (*Kanji*). The Nikkei Sangyo newspaper reports that from insurance payments, accounting, human resource management, to patents, Chinese workers have advantages in handling these documents, and in performing at a low rate of typos, which is 0.01% among Chinese workers, whereas it is 10% among Japanese workers.

Taking the report of IPA (2011) into account, this chapter assumes that countries and country groups provide certain business processes as shown in Table 5–1. First, in order to identify the differences between high-cost countries and low-cost countries, OECD and non-OECD are identified. Among non-OECD counties, China is identified because of the unique characteristics of lingual proximity as stated above. India is also identified because it has a growing software and information services industry, and it is the major exporter of computer and information services to the U.S. (Takagi 2011). The category of ASEAN 6 is identified to include Indonesia, Malaysia, the Philippines, Singapore, Thailand, and Vietnam, as shown in Table 5–2. Only these 6 countries are included because of data availability, but note that Singapore, which is advanced in terms of utilizing information technology, represents the major part of the information services trade with Japan among these 6 countries. The U.S. is also identified, because it is one of the central markets for information services. This chapter considers the exporting countries and country groups as the proxies of business processes which are outsourced to each country and country group. By relating countries and outsourced business processes, this chapter

Table 5–1. The relation of countries and the outsourced business process

	R&D	Consulting & Strategy	Architecture Design	Program Design	Program Development	Testing	Operation	Cloud computing	BPO
OECD	○	—	—	—	—	—	—	○	—
Non-OECD	—	—	—	○	○	○	○	—	○
China	—	—	—	○	○	○	○	—	○
India	△	—	—	○	○	○	○	—	○
ASEAN 6	△	—	—	○	○	○	○	△	○
U.S.	○	—	—	—	—	—	—	○	—

○ Countries that focus on providing the business processes. △ Countries that do not focus on the business processes, but provide the business processes.
— Countries that do not provide the business processes.

82 Information Technology and the Japanese Economy

Table 5–2. Exporting countries and country groups in the analysis

Country / Country group	Notes
OECD	Australia, Belgium, Canada, France, Germany, Italy, Korea, Luxembourg, Mexico, Netherlands, New Zealand, Spain, Sweden, Switzerland, UK, U.S.
Non-OECD	Brazil, Cayman Islands, China, Hong Kong, India, Indonesia, Iran, Malaysia, Philippines, Russia, Saudi Arabia, Singapore, South Africa, Thailand, UAE, Vietnam
ASEAN 6	Indonesia, Malaysia, Philippines, Singapore, Thailand, Vietnam
China	China
India	India
U.S.	United States

addresses the question of how outsourcing to certain countries, in other words, the outsourcing of certain services, affects employment in Japan.

5.2 Measurement Methodology

This analysis applies a similar approach as Takagi and Tanaka (2012c) to estimate the outsourcing of information services, but specifies the countries which export information services to Japan.

This analysis calculates the amount of offshore outsourcing from the input-output table following Falk and Walfmayr (2008). The input-output table is obtained from a JIP 2009 database (RIETI 2009). Two types of offshoring are defined in this analysis. The first is "traditional outsourcing," which is assessed as imported intermediate inputs in the same industry. It is called "traditional outsourcing" because it typically assesses the outsourcing of manufacturing goods which are imported from overseas and sold to a domestic industry which is in the same industrial sector. Because the imported product is sold to the same industry, it is assumed that the domestic industry is outsourcing the production process overseas. This idea of measurement was first introduced by Feenstra and Hanson (1997, 1999),[4] and subsequently applied by Falk and Walf-

---
4 Falk and Walfmayr (2008)

mayr (2008). The calculation of traditional outsourcing is described as follows:

Traditional outsourcing of goods i =

$$[\text{input purchases of good } j \text{ by goods } i] * \left[\frac{\text{imports of good } j}{\text{total domestic demand of good } j} \right]$$

where $i = j$. (5–1)

Traditional outsourcing of industry i is calculated as input purchases of good j by industry i times the import ratio of industry j (imports of good j divided by the total domestic demand of good j).

The second type of outsourcing is "information services outsourcing". This is assessed as imported intermediate inputs of "information services" for each industry. The calculation is described as follows:

Information services outsourcing of industry i=

$$[\text{imput purchases of information services by industry } i] * \left[\frac{\text{imports of information services}}{\text{total domestic demand of information services}} \right]$$

(5–2)

Information services outsourcing of industry i is calculated as input purchases of information services by industry i times the import ratio of information services (imports of information services divided by total domestic demand of information services). This measurement follows a similar approach as traditional outsourcing, but specifically focuses on the outsourcing of information services.

The JIP2009 database provides the share of 32 countries and regions which export information services to Japan each year.

Therefore, the amounts of imports from each country are calculated by multiplying the total amount by the share of each country. Because China, India, and the U.S. have a significant presence as exporters to Japan, imports from those countries are specified.[5] Imports from country groups such as the OECD and ASEAN 6 are also calculated. Only countries whose data is available in the JIP 2009 are included in the analysis. The exporting countries and country groups which are assessed in the analysis are summarized in Table 5-2.

There are several limitations in this measurement of outsourcing. First, the same import ratio is applied to all industries and also to final consumption. In some industries, import might be designated mostly to final consumption, and in others, import might be designated to the intermediate input of a specific industry. Because it is impossible to distinguish the weight of imports across the industries as well as final consumption, the same import ratio is applied for all industries.

Second, it is impossible to capture outsourced production which is exported to other countries. Suppose that a product is manufactured in a foreign country under a Japanese company's control, then exported to a third-party country. This transaction does not appear on the input-output table of the Japanese economy.

Third, it is also impossible to distinguish between foreign production under the control of a Japanese purchaser and production under foreign control. If some imported intermediate product is manufactured under a Japanese company's control, it is easily called outsourcing. However, if the imported intermediate product is produced under the control of the exporting country, it is not as clear as in the former case to call it outsourcing. There is no clear line to distinguish outsourcing based on the extent of domestic control, and various types of production might be included in the measurement.

However, given the difficulty in measuring offshore outsourcing,

---

5 Liu and Trefler (2008) focus more specifically on trade with China and India, because public concern is concentrated on trade with these two countries.

it is still meaningful to conduct analyses with the best available data and measurement methodology. Major prior studies also employ the same approach by considering the same limitations. Therefore, this research also uses this approach, thus enabling comparison with prior studies.

5.3 Outsourcing Trends

Figure 5–2 shows the trend of the absolute value of import from each country and country group. Although there is a fluctuation in the period, it shows the general trend of increase in the amount from most countries.

Figure 5–3 shows the trend of the share of countries which export information services to Japan. It shows that the general trend of import from high-cost countries has declined, and import from low-cost countries has increased throughout the period. Particularly, the share of the U.S. surpassed 60% in the late 1990s, but it has fallen to below 50% in the mid-2000s. On the other hand, import from non-OECD countries increased during the same period. In particular, China increased its share from less than 1.7% in 1996 to around 9.1% in 2006.

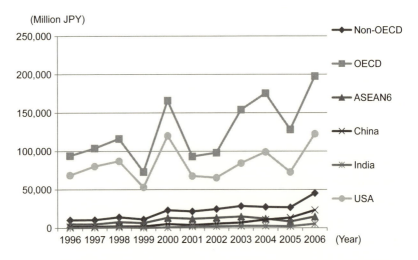

Figure 5–2. Trend of value of imports from source countries (million JPY)
Source: JIP 2009 database (RIETI 2009)

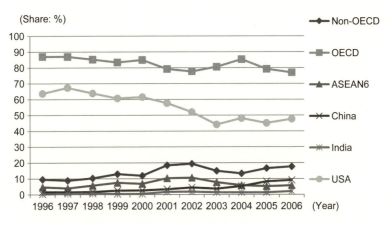

Figure 5–3. Trend of share of exporting countries
Source: JIP 2009 database (RIETI 2009)

5.4 Estimation of the Effect on Employment

This section assesses the effect of the outsourcing of information services to specific countries or regions on employment in Japan. By using the amount of offshore outsourcing obtained in the previous sections, this section estimates the effect by panel data analysis.

5.4.1 Estimation models

The estimation model is based on the conventional labor demand model and is described as follows:

$$\Delta L_{it} = a_0 + a_1 \Delta Y_{it} + a_2 \Delta W_{it} + a_3 \Delta TDO_{it} + a_4 \Delta ITinv_{it} + a_c \Delta SER_{cit} + v_i + e_{it} \qquad (5\text{--}3)$$

where delta is the ratio from the previous year, i is industry, t is year. L is employment, Y denotes value added, and W is real wage. TDO denotes traditional outsourcing. SER denotes information services outsourcing which is decomposed into each country and region, c. The combination of countries and regions is selected to avoid duplication. The error term is divided into industry effect as v_i and error term e_{it}. The effect is estimated for all industries, manufacturing industries, and service industries separately.

Lagged variation is derived from the estimation model 5–3. The estimation model 5–3 assesses the contemporaneous effect of outsourcing on employment. However, it may take awhile until the transition of the business process is settled and those transitions actually affect employment. In the lagged model, outsourcing variables of one year before the dependent variables are used as explanatory variables. Similarly, the lagged data of Y is also used because companies might react to the expansion of output by overtime work in the first year, and they may hire more employees the next year. The lagged data of W is also used because it might also take time until the variation of wages affects employment. The lagged model is described as follows:

$$\Delta L_{it} = a_0 + a_1\Delta Y_{it-1} + a_2\Delta W_{it-1} + a_3\Delta TDO_{it-1} + a_4\Delta ITinv_{it-1} +$$
$$a_c\Delta SER_{cit} + v_i + e_{it} \tag{5-4}$$

Year coverage is 5 years from 2002 to 2006. In Japan, offshore outsourcing of information services became popular around this period. To compare the results with more previous years, the analysis is also applied to a data set which covers 1998 to 2001. During this period, offshore outsourcing became popular in the U.S. because of the labor shortage needed to address the Y2K issue, but offshore outsourcing was not so popular in Japan.

The estimation has four variations for the combination of explanatory variables. Variation 1 uses total information services outsourcing without country specification. Variation 2 decomposes exporting countries into the OECD and Non-OECD countries. Variation 3 decomposes Non-OECD countries to China, India, and ASEAN 6 countries. Variation 4 uses the U.S. instead of OECD countries.

In the estimation of coefficients, the fixed effect model is employed for the following reasons. First, either a fixed or random effect model has to be selected throughout the contemporaneous and the lagged model in order to make a comparison across these multiple models. Secondly, it is assumed that each firm has a relatively stable and unique adaptability to offshore outsourcing. For these reasons, the fixed effect model is employed both on the contemporaneous and the lagged model.[6]

The summary of statistics is shown in Appendix 5–A and the correlation matrix is shown in Appendix 5–B. The outlier is eliminated once from the dataset by the standard in which values

---

6 The results of the Hausman test are shown in Tables 4–3 and 4–4, which were conducted with the sigmamore option using STATA/IC 11.2. Generally, the fixed effect model is supported for "All Industries" and "Manufacturing", and the random effect model is supported for "Services", but the fixed effect model is employed throughout the analyses based on the reasons stated in this section. Estimation with the random effect model is also applied on the specification that the fixed effect model is less applicable such as in [1] to [4] of the service sector in Table 4–3 and in [1] to [4] of the service sector in Table 4–4, but the results do not affect the following discussion.

are within the means plus/minus four standard deviations.

5.4.2 Results

Table 5–3 and Table 5–4 show the results of the estimation. The estimation was conducted using STATA/IC 11.2. Because it is assumed that it takes awhile until the increase of outsourcing affects employment, the following discussion is based on the lagged model in Table 5–4.

First, significant effects of information services outsourcing are found in coefficients in the manufacturing sector. There is no significant effect in the service sector, and the adjusted R-squared is also higher in the manufacturing sector than in the service sector.

Focusing on manufacturing sector, variation 1 shows that information services outsourcing as a total has a negative effect on employment. By decomposing the exporting countries into OECD and non-OECD countries in variation 2, outsourcing to OECD countries has a negative effect on employment, and outsourcing to non-OECD countries has no significant effect. However, if non-OECD countries are further decomposed into China, India, and ASEAN 6 in variation 3, outsourcing to China has a positive effect, while India and ASEAN 6 have negative effects on manufacturing employment. In variation 4 outsourcing to the U.S. has almost the same negative effect as the OECD.

In terms of comparison with the contemporaneous model in Table 5–3, the negative effect of outsourcing to OECD countries in the lagged model is also detected in the contemporaneous model in Table 5–3. However, the negative effect of outsourcing to India was positive in the contemporaneous model.

5.5 Discussion

The first feature of the results is that information services outsourcing affects the manufacturing sector, not the service sector. This effect has already been pointed out in Takagi and Tanaka (2012c). This result indicates the following possibilities. Although informa-

Table 5–3. Results of estimation (Contemporaneous model), 2002–2006

	All Industries				Manufacturing				Services			
	[1]	[2]	[3]	[4]	[1]	[2]	[3]	[4]	[1]	[2]	[3]	[4]
Wage	0.080	0.065	0.084	0.085	0.189**	0.175***	0.274***	0.278***	0.027	0.017	0.003	0.003
	(0.062)	(0.055)	(0.072)	(0.071)	(0.079)	(0.064)	(0.077)	(0.078)	(0.089)	(0.085)	(0.088)	(0.089)
Value added	0.016	0.025	0.010	0.011	0.020	0.038**	0.016	0.019	−0.032	−0.030	−0.055	−0.056
	(0.017)	(0.016)	(0.015)	(0.015)	(0.018)	(0.017)	(0.016)	(0.016)	(0.040)	(0.042)	(0.047)	(0.047)
Traditional outsourcing	0.007	0.011	0.003	0.004	0.014	0.022	−0.004	−0.003	0.010	0.010	0.012	0.012
	(0.009)	(0.009)	(0.008)	(0.008)	(0.015)	(0.013)	(0.014)	(0.014)	(0.009)	(0.009)	(0.010)	(0.010)
IT investment	−0.001	−0.009	−0.005	−0.006	0.014	−0.001	0.014	0.012	0.007	0.007	0.003	0.003
	(0.010)	(0.009)	(0.010)	(0.010)	(0.011)	(0.010)	(0.012)	(0.012)	(0.015)	(0.015)	(0.012)	(0.012)
Information services outsourcing	0.025***				0.040***				0.003			
	(0.005)				(0.007)				(0.008)			
To:												
OECD		−0.014**	0.002			−0.021***	0.001			−0.002	0.003	
		(0.007)	(0.008)			(0.007)	(0.009)			(0.013)	(0.013)	
Non-OECD		0.058***				0.084***				0.008		
		(0.008)				(0.008)				(0.015)		
China			−0.008	−0.006			−0.004	−0.001			−0.017	−0.019
			(0.017)	(0.017)			(0.023)	(0.024)			(0.023)	(0.019)
India			0.087***	0.087***			0.126***	0.126***			0.039**	0.037
			(0.015)	(0.015)			(0.023)	(0.021)			(0.017)	(0.023)
ASEAN 6			−0.104***	−0.101***			−0.155***	−0.150***			−0.050***	−0.048***
			(0.019)	(0.018)			(0.033)	(0.030)			(0.012)	(0.016)
U.S.				−0.004				−0.006				0.005
				(0.013)				(0.013)				(0.021)
constant	0.849***	0.838***	0.900***	0.899***	0.688***	0.667***	0.679***	0.673***	0.980***	0.985***	1.060***	1.061***
	(0.068)	(0.061)	(0.087)	(0.086)	(0.093)	(0.076)	(0.094)	(0.095)	(0.086)	(0.082)	(0.109)	(0.107)
N	408	408	408	408	245	245	245	245	135	135	135	135
R^2 (Within)	0.074	0.175	0.250	0.250	0.161	0.349	0.479	0.479	0.026	0.029	0.078	0.078
Adjusted R^2	0.330	0.401	0.452	0.452	0.394	0.527	0.617	0.618	0.262	0.257	0.280	0.280
Hausman test	17.14	17.19	29.93	29.92	18.66	24.79	31.52	30.32	2.51	2.71	5.32	5.27
χ^2 (p)	(0.0042)	(0.0086)	(0.0002)	(0.0002)	(0.0022)	(0.0004)	(0.0001)	(0.0002)	(0.7750)	(0.8441)	(0.7225)	(0.7288)

Robust standard errors in parentheses. * $p<0.10$ ** $p<0.05$ *** $p<0.01$. Adjusted R-squared are calculated by least-squares dummy-variables regression.

Table 5–4. Results of estimation (Lagged model), 2002–2006

	All Industries				Manufacturing				Services			
	[1]	[2]	[3]	[4]	[1]	[2]	[3]	[4]	[1]	[2]	[3]	[4]
Wage	0.285***	0.282***	0.186**	0.186**	0.514***	0.500***	0.291***	0.282***	0.234**	0.241**	0.198**	0.198**
	(0.079)	(0.081)	(0.078)	(0.078)	(0.073)	(0.074)	(0.059)	(0.058)	(0.093)	(0.097)	(0.076)	(0.076)
Value added	0.064***	0.064***	0.036*	0.037*	0.059**	0.060**	0.031	0.031	-0.049	-0.052	-0.073	-0.073
	(0.023)	(0.023)	(0.022)	(0.022)	(0.024)	(0.024)	(0.020)	(0.020)	(0.050)	(0.049)	(0.057)	(0.057)
Traditional outsourcing	0.010*	0.011*	0.004	0.004	0.024**	0.026**	0.014*	0.014*	-0.000	-0.000	-0.001	-0.001
	(0.006)	(0.006)	(0.006)	(0.006)	(0.012)	(0.012)	(0.008)	(0.008)	(0.005)	(0.005)	(0.006)	(0.006)
IT investment	0.016*	0.016*	0.006	0.006	0.010	0.009	-0.024**	-0.025**	0.018	0.017	0.022*	0.022*
	(0.008)	(0.009)	(0.009)	(0.009)	(0.009)	(0.010)	(0.010)	(0.010)	(0.014)	(0.014)	(0.013)	(0.013)
Information services outsourcing To:	-0.007				-0.023***				0.005			
OECD	(0.005)				(0.008)				(0.005)			
		-0.008	-0.011*			-0.021**	-0.034***			0.009	0.007	
		(0.006)	(0.006)			(0.010)	(0.010)			(0.006)	(0.008)	
Non-OECD		0.006				0.006				-0.020		
		(0.020)				(0.031)				(0.029)		
China			0.016	0.025*			0.027*	0.051***			-0.011	-0.014
			(0.012)	(0.013)			(0.016)	(0.019)			(0.018)	(0.017)
India			-0.015**	-0.013**			-0.026**	-0.020**			-0.010	-0.011
			(0.006)	(0.006)			(0.008)	(0.008)			(0.008)	(0.008)
ASEAN 6			-0.030**	-0.032***			-0.029*	-0.041***			-0.010	-0.007
			(0.013)	(0.012)			(0.015)	(0.013)			(0.025)	(0.023)
U.S.				-0.019**				-0.051***				0.008
				(0.008)				(0.014)				(0.011)
constant	0.612***	0.609***	0.788***	0.783***	0.387***	0.393***	0.727***	0.725***	0.793***	0.807***	0.885***	0.886***
	(0.068)	(0.067)	(0.076)	(0.076)	(0.070)	(0.069)	(0.071)	(0.072)	(0.089)	(0.094)	(0.098)	(0.098)
N	404	404	404	404	241	241	241	241	136	136	136	136
R^2 (Within)	0.135	0.137	0.281	0.283	0.234	0.236	0.516	0.521	0.138	0.144	0.186	0.185
Adjusted R^2	0.385	0.383	0.483	0.485	0.453	0.452	0.649	0.652	0.382	0.380	0.399	0.398
Hausman test	17.86	17.02	24.02	23.37	17.20	16.61	27.85	26.54	5.53	5.43	6.59	6.64
χ^2 (p)	(0.0031)	(0.0092)	(0.0023)	(0.0029)	(0.0041)	(0.0108)	(0.0005)	(0.0008)	(0.3546)	(0.4902)	(0.5814)	(0.5761)

Robust standard errors in parentheses. * $p<0.10$ ** $p<0.05$ *** $p<0.01$. Adjusted R-squared are calculated by least-squares dummy-variables regression.

tion services are one of the service industries, the actual business of information services is also used in the manufacturing sector. Because recent manufacturing products include many software and after-service components, information services outsourcing affects the manufacturing sector. Information services in the manufacturing sector are far from its core-competence; therefore, outsourcing might have affected employment in the manufacturing sector.

Significant results in the manufacturing sector with country specification in the lagged model suggest interesting possibilities. Results in the variation of the decomposed countries in the OECD and non-OECD [2], and the U.S. and other countries [4], show that outsourcing to high-cost and developed countries substitutes for employment in Japan. It is reasonable to suppose that the skills and costs of labor in Japan are similar to other OECD countries. Therefore, outsourcing to those countries might reduce employment in Japan. Falk and Walfmayr (2008), who specify outsourcing to high-wage and low-wage countries from the EU countries, found that imports from low-wage countries have significant and negative effects on employment in the service sector. The results shown in this chapter contradict the results of Falk and Walfmayr (2008) in terms of the different effect of the outsourcing to high-wage and low-wage countries.

One of the important findings in this analysis is that outsourcing to Asia is not homogenous across countries. First, outsourcing to China seems to complement employment in Japan. Because the skills and cost of labor in China are significantly different from those in Japan, outsourcing to China might contribute to the growth of industry in Japan. In addition to the differences, geographical or language proximity between China and Japan as discussed in section 5–1 would also explain the benefit of outsourcing to China.

On the other hand, outsourcing to India substitutes for employment in Japan. India is a major exporter of computing and information services to the U.S., but the amount of offshore outsourcing from Japan to India is very limited compared to China, as seen in Figure 5–2. This might be due to the difference of language, geographical distance, and general experience of cooperation in business. In terms of negative effects, India is increasing services of highly skilled process such as R&D (IPA 2011). These highly skilled processes can serve as a substitute for such processes in Japan.

The reason for the negative effect of outsourcing to ASEAN 6 is not clear, but Singapore, which provides high-cost and highly skilled services is included in the ASEAN 6 countries. More than half of ASEAN6's share of information services outsourcing is to Singapore, so this might have affected employment in Japan for the same reason as the OECD and the U.S.

Most of the significant effects of information services outsourcing are not found in the previous period, 1998–2001. Because offshore outsourcing became popular after this period in Japan, significant effects on employment can be seen as effects through the increase of the offshore outsourcing of information services.

As stated in the introduction, this chapter assumes that the OECD and the U.S. provide R&D or cloud computing. On the other hand, China, India, and ASEAN 6 mainly focus on software development processes such as program design to operation, and Business Process Outsourcing, although India and Singapore also have the possibility to provide R&D and cloud computing. If this becomes the case, the outsourcing of R&D and cloud computing will reduce manufacturing employment in Japan, and the outsourcing of software development processes will increase manufacturing employment in Japan.

However, the positive effect of offshore outsourcing of software development on employment is not necessarily applicable in the future. As seen in Chapter 3, the standardization of businesses and the development of communication networks are promoting cloud computing. Cloud computing is an alternative to customized software, but software development processes are still required to construct cloud computing services. Cloud computing providers need to construct and continuously improve their own services to meet the demands of customers and various social requirements. These software development processes for cloud computing would need the best available skills to compete against other providers globally. Therefore, when the software development process is used for constructing cloud computing, in-house development rather than offshore outsourcing would be more required and rationalized in terms of flexibility and agility.

Related to this point, it is inferred from the results that outsourcing of R&D and cloud computing reduces employment in Japan, which would lead to the reduction of high-skilled labour in the field. This might reduce not only employment in Japan, but also the innovation capability of the Japanese information industry. If this were to be the case, promoting R&D in domestic entities and locating data centers in Japan would be one of the options to consider as public policy. Taking into consideration the above argument on software development for cloud computing, empirical results should be interpreted by considering the development of technology and business models. For instance, there would be diverse skills and roles in software development, and a part of them might be an important element for other sources of growth in the future.

5.6 Conclusion

This chapter provided statistical evidence to assess the effect of offshore outsourcing on employment in Japan, specifying the differences across trading partners. The analysis revealed that the effect is diverse depending on trading partners, particularly when decomposing trading partners to China, India, and ASEAN 6. Outsourcing to China appears to increase employment in Japan, and outsourcing to India and ASEAN 6 reduces employment in Japan.

Interpreting these results on business processes, outsourcing of highly skilled services such as R&D and cloud computing seems to reduce manufacturing employment in Japan, and outsourcing of software development processes increases manufacturing employment in Japan. Analysis on organizational view in Chapter 3 suggested that transaction costs are lower and easier to outsource for cloud computing than software development or business process outsourcing. If the offshore outsourcing of cloud computing can reduce employment in Japan, being concerned about what information services can be standardized and packaged as cloud computing services is worth thinking about, as is what fraction among them would be provided from overseas, in order to estimate the current and future effect on the economy. Compared to prior studies in other countries, Amiti and Wei (2005) suggested that information services outsourcing does not have a negative effect on employment in the UK. They explained that an insignificant result is because there is job creation in the same industry classification that supplements job reduction due to the outsourcing. On the other hand, Falk and Wolfmayr (2008) suggest service outsourcing to low-wage countries has a significant negative effect on service employment in EU countries. However, they suggest that this effect is not significant when they focus only on "business services." Based on the methodologies of these prior studies, this study conducted a more detailed analysis on the exporting countries and found some results that contradict the prior studies. Particularly, this study shows the possibility that information services outsourcing has effects on employment in the manufacturing sector, and the effect is different depending on to which country the business process is outsourced.

However, there are several limitations and future challenge in this analysis. As stated in previous sections, there are limitations on the measurement of outsourcing. The years of coverage in this analysis are from 2002 to 2006, which covers the period after the emerging popularity of offshore outsourcing and before the global financial crisis. If a comparison with analysis on and after 2007 were conducted, it would be possible to identify the difference of the effects on industrial structure before and after the financial crisis. In addition, the exploration on occupations which are affected by outsourcing should provide insightful information to understand the effect of outsourcing on industrial composition and to present policy implications.

The analysis in this chapter revealed that offshore outsourcing of information services suggests downward pressure on employment, although its effect is different across trading partners. In order to discuss the comprehensive effect of offshore outsourcing on the economy, it is necessary to analyze the effect also on productivity. If offshore outsourcing reduces employment and productivity is not affected or declines, the overall effect on the economy would be shrinkage. Conversely, if productivity is raised by offshore outsourcing, this productivity growth would make the output of the Japanese economy at least sustained, or lead to growth by making the industry competitive in the global market. In order to find the comprehensive effect on the economy, the next chapter assesses the impact of offshore outsourcing on the productivity of the Japanese economy.

Appendix 5–A. Summary of statistics, 2002–2006

Variable	N	Mean	Standard Deviation	Min	Max
ΔEmployment	408	0.983	0.043	0.811	1.177
ΔWage	408	1.010	0.037	0.860	1.238
ΔValue added	408	1.016	0.142	0.099	1.781
ΔTraditional outsourcing	408	1.067	0.233	0.160	2.486
ΔIT investment	408	1.080	0.232	0.142	2.094
ΔInformation services outsourcing	408	1.200	0.303	0.575	2.034
To:					
ΔOECD	408	1.200	0.319	0.535	2.111
ΔNon-OECD	408	1.178	0.267	0.717	1.745
ΔChina	408	1.431	0.201	0.894	1.902
ΔIndia	408	1.301	0.576	0.587	2.528
ΔASEAN 6	408	1.088	0.366	0.510	1.816
ΔU.S.	408	1.161	0.316	0.539	1.732

Appendix 5–B. Correlation matrix, 2002–2006

	Employment	Wage	Value added	Traditional outsourcing	IT investment	Information services outsourcing	OECD	Non-OECD	China	India	ASEAN 6	U.S.
Employment	1											
Wage	0.033	1										
Value added	0.048	0.058	1									
Traditional outsourcing	0.110**	−0.048	0.052	1								
IT investment	0.02	−0.099**	0.014	0.018	1							
Information services outsourcing	0.233***	0.117**	0.028	0.051	−0.120**	1						
OECD	0.200***	0.101**	0.035	0.066	−0.129***	0.988***	1					
Non-OECD	0.331***	0.095*	−0.018	0.016	−0.009	0.775***	0.675***	1				
China	0.310***	−0.115**	−0.042	0.153***	0.101**	0.522***	0.479***	0.729***	1			
India	0.309***	0.064	0	0.025	0.006	0.777***	0.692***	0.971***	0.782***	1		
ASEAN 6	0.253***	0.066	−0.02	0.001	0	0.832***	0.748***	0.974***	0.708***	0.965***	1	
U.S.	0.290***	0.045	0.024	0.092*	−0.05	0.923***	0.901***	0.837***	0.772***	0.896***	0.870***	1

* $p<0.10$, ** $p<0.05$, *** $p<0.01$. Listwise.

CHAPTER 6
Offshore Outsourcing of Information Services and Productivity

The previous chapter assessed the impact of offshore outsourcing of information services on Japanese employment. This chapter turns to the effect on productivity, following the same framework as in Chapter 5. This chapter provides an empirical assessment on the effects of information services outsourcing on Total Factor Productivity in Japan with a specific focus on trading partners and outsourced business processes. The results show that the manufacturing sector gains positive effects from outsourcing to a wider range of countries than the service sector. This section discusses the results in relation to outsourced business processes and productivity growth in Japan.[1]

6.1 Introduction

As shown in Chapter 2, prior studies of empirical analysis on the effects of offshore outsourcing are relatively limited, and most of the prior studies have concentrated on the effect on employment (Amiti and Wei 2005, Falk and Wolfmayr 2008, Liu and Trefler 2008, Takagi and Tanaka 2012c). However, productivity is also assumed to be affected by offshore outsourcing because it affects the cost share of intermediate inputs and technology to utilize inputs. Only Amiti and Wei (2009) have directly analyzed this point and they found that the offshore outsourcing of services has a positive effect on the total factor productivity (TFP) in the United States.

This study assumes that productivity would be raised by offshore

---

[1] This chapter is based on Takagi and Tanaka (2012a), which is restructured and revised for this book.

outsourcing in three ways: cost effect, business process re-engineering (BPR) effect, and core-competence effect. In cost effect, outsourcing reduces the cost of the intermediate input of information services. Until competitors also reduce costs and the prices of final products or services reach a lower equilibrium, companies that outsource information services can benefit from cost reduction and achieve higher profits. Second, in the process of organizing outsourcing, the business processes which are to be outsourced are reviewed, simplified, and optimized. This BPR process also will raise productivity. Finally, companies can focus on the core competence of organizations by outsourcing. However, this effect would take several years because of the educational and structural change of workers. If productivity is raised by offshore outsourcing, it will make the industry grow in the long term and will even support employment in the future.

Although prior studies that directly assess the effect of information services outsourcing are limited, related studies on productivity such as Motohashi (2005), Jorgenson and Motohashi (2005), Nakanishi and Inui (2008) are taken into consideration. In sum, this research is based on prior studies of offshore outsourcing and employment in terms of the field of study and also on productivity studies in terms of the method and analytical framework.

6.2 Trend of Variables

Figure 6–1 shows the average growth of TFP excluding government services which is calculated from the JIP 2009 database (RIETI 2009). The score is standardized at 1980 equals 1. TFP growth in the manufacturing sector had been stagnate since the late 1990s, but has generally grown throughout the period. Fukao and Kwon (2006) stated that the slowdown in the 1990s was because the reallocation of resources from less efficient to more efficient firms was very slow and limited. Conversely, productivity in the service sector decreased for most of the period, except after 2002, when TFP began to increase. The trend of the volume and share of countries

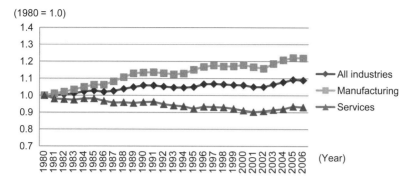

Figure 6–1. TFP trend (1980 = 1.0)
Source: JIP 2009 database (RIETI 2009)

that export information services to Japan is the same as in Figures 5–2 and 5–3 in Chapter 5.

6.3 Estimation of the Effect on TFP

This section assesses the effect of outsourcing of information services to specific countries or regions on total factor productivity in Japan. By using the amount of offshore outsourcing obtained in Chapter 5 and TFP data calculated in the previous section, this section estimates the effect by panel data analysis.

6.3.1 Estimation models

Studies on productivity commonly use the output of a firm or industry as a dependent variable, based on production function (Amiti and Wei 2009, Jorgenson and Motohashi 2005, Motohashi 2005). The other approach is to use TFP data that are already available as dependent variables and to assess several explanatory variables that are not used explicitly in the production function to calculate TFP. Nakanishi and Inui (2008) used this approach. This study employs a similar approach, using TFP data as dependent variables. The estimation model is panel data analysis and is described as follows:

$$\Delta TFP_{it} = \alpha + \beta_1 \Delta \frac{TDO_{it}}{Y_{it}} + \beta_2 \Delta \frac{SER_{cit}}{Y_{it}} + \beta_3 \Delta \frac{IT_{it}}{Y_{it}} + v_i + e_{it} \qquad (6-1)$$

where delta represents the ratio from the previous year, TFP is total factor productivity (as indicated in the JIP database (RIETI 2009), TDO is traditional outsourcing, and SER is information services outsourcing decomposed to each country and region, c. IT denotes information technology stock, i the industry sector, and t, year. All explanatory variables are divided by output because intermediate inputs are usually considered in the process of calculating TFP.

IT stock is also included in the analysis as an explanatory variable because potentially, IT stock may affect TFP in two channels. In the first channel, utilization of IT affects productivity directly because software and information systems make the business process efficient. In the second channel, IT promotes outsourcing both in traditional and information services, and in this case, the outsourcing affects productivity. The exporting countries and country groups assessed in the analysis are the same as in Table 5–2 in Chapter 5.

Lagged analysis is also conducted because it may take awhile until outsourcing affects productivity. Cost effect and BPR effect would affect TFP in a relatively short period of time because these effects are usually realized at the same time as any increase in outsourcing. On the other hand, the core-competence effect would take a longer time because it may take a while for firms to arrange their organizational structures. IT stock affects TFP in a relatively short period of time because business process would be optimized at the same time as the introduction of new IT systems. Therefore, the IT stock in the explanatory variable is not lagged. The lagged model is described as follows:

$$\Delta TFP_{it} = \alpha + \beta_1 \Delta \frac{TDO_{it-1}}{Y_{it-1}} + \beta_2 \Delta \frac{SER_{cit-1}}{Y_{it-1}} + \beta_3 \Delta \frac{IT_{it}}{Y_{it}} + v_i + e_{it} \qquad (6-2)$$

The fixed-effects model is employed to estimate coefficients for the same reason as explained in section 5.4.1.[2] All data for this anal-

---

2 The results of Hausman test are shown in Tables 6–1 and 6–2, which are conducted with the sigmamore option using STATA/IC 11.2. Generally, the fixed effect model

ysis were obtained from the JIP database (RIETI 2009) and employ 108 industry classifications. Government services are excluded from this analysis, and all variables are real value. The JIP database covers from 1970 to 2006 for most tables, but the latest five years (2002–2006) are used in the present analysis to control for the change of industrial structure. Outliers are eliminated once based on the standard, which is means plus/minus four times the standard deviations from the 1998–2006 dataset. The summary and correlations of variables are shown in Appendix 6–A and 6–B, respectively. Multicollinearity is not detected in either the contemporaneous or lagged model.

6.3.2 Results

Table 6–1 shows the results of estimation of the contemporaneous model. Generally, information services outsourcing has negative effects on TFP, except for outsourcing to India. In the manufacturing sector, outsourcing to non-OECD, China, and ASEAN 6 countries has negative effects on TFP. In the service sector, outsourcing to non-OECD and China also has negative effects. Outsourcing to India has a positive effect only in the manufacturing sector. In the results of the lagged model in Table 6–2, information services outsourcing to most of the countries has positive effects on TFP. In the manufacturing sector, outsourcing to OECD, China, and the United States has positive effects, whereas outsourcing to ASEAN 6 countries has a negative effect. In the service sector, outsourcing only to China and India has a positive effect.

In terms of IT stocks, the increase of IT stocks has a negative effect on TFP in both models in most specifications. The adjusted R-squared is higher in the contemporaneous model than in the lagged model.

---

is supported for most of the specification, despite some exception. The fixed effect model is employed throughout the analyses based on the same reason stated in section 5.4.1. Estimation with the random effect model is also applied on the specification in which the fixed effect model is less applicable such as in [1], [3], and [4] of service sector in Table 6–1 and [1] and [2] of the service sector in Table 6–2, but the results do not affect the following discussion.

Table 6–1. Results of estimation (Contemporaneous model), 2002–2006

	All industries				Manufacturing				Services			
	[1]	[2]	[3]	[4]	[1]	[2]	[3]	[4]	[1]	[2]	[3]	[4]
ΔTDO	-0.023*	-0.023**	-0.013	-0.013	-0.021	-0.023*	-0.010	-0.011	-0.022	-0.018	-0.012	-0.012
	(0.012)	(0.011)	(0.009)	(0.009)	(0.014)	(0.013)	(0.009)	(0.009)	(0.018)	(0.017)	(0.013)	(0.013)
ΔIT Stock	-0.189***	-0.168***	-0.177***	-0.175***	-0.203***	-0.173***	-0.185***	-0.181***	-0.121*	-0.124**	-0.140**	-0.140**
	(0.038)	(0.035)	(0.033)	(0.034)	(0.042)	(0.045)	(0.037)	(0.038)	(0.070)	(0.060)	(0.057)	(0.056)
ΔSER	-0.030***				-0.028***				-0.027***			
	(0.007)				(0.010)				(0.009)			
To:												
OECD		-0.012	-0.013**			-0.012	-0.011			0.001	-0.006	
		(0.008)	(0.006)			(0.011)	(0.010)			(0.013)	(0.011)	
Non-OECD		-0.036***				-0.034***				-0.049***		
		(0.008)				(0.011)				(0.016)		
China			-0.085***	-0.081***			-0.090***	-0.088***			-0.073***	-0.072***
			(0.011)	(0.011)			(0.010)	(0.012)			(0.014)	(0.013)
India			0.060***	0.067***			0.099***	0.105***			-0.006	-0.003
			(0.014)	(0.016)			(0.010)	(0.015)			(0.020)	(0.026)
ASEAN 6			-0.071***	-0.082***			-0.127***	-0.136***			0.012	0.006
			(0.018)	(0.020)			(0.014)	(0.018)			(0.025)	(0.029)
U.S.				-0.014				-0.010				-0.004
				(0.010)				(0.015)				(0.019)
constant	1.263***	1.263***	1.341***	1.337***	1.277***	1.270***	1.365***	1.359***	1.186***	1.210***	1.268***	1.266***
	(0.043)	(0.039)	(0.039)	(0.039)	(0.059)	(0.056)	(0.049)	(0.049)	(0.065)	(0.057)	(0.054)	(0.054)
N	407	407	407	407	243	243	243	243	134	134	134	134
R^2 (Within)	0.208	0.320	0.478	0.474	0.209	0.341	0.612	0.609	0.174	0.277	0.364	0.363
Adjusted R^2	0.410	0.492	0.607	0.605	0.462	0.549	0.732	0.730	0.370	0.443	0.500	0.499
Hausman test	46.73	34.42	16.93	18.41	68.55	30.57	15.08	16.15	5.19	9.25	8.08	8.30
χ^2 (p)	(0.0000)	(0.0000)	(0.0095)	(0.0053)	(0.0000)	(0.0000)	(0.0197)	(0.0130)	(0.1586)	(0.0552)	(0.2324)	(0.2169)

Robust standard errors in parentheses. * $p < 0.10$; ** $p < 0.05$; *** $p < 0.01$. Adjusted R-squared are calculated by least-squares dummy-variables regression. The number of "All industries" does not match the sum of manufacturing and services because "All industries" includes other industries such as primary industries and non-classified industries.

Table 6-2. Results of estimation (Lagged model), 2002–2006

	All industries				Manufacturing				Services			
	[1]	[2]	[3]	[4]	[1]	[2]	[3]	[4]	[1]	[2]	[3]	[4]
ΔTDO	0.020**	0.018**	0.014*	0.015*	0.012	0.011	0.004	0.004	0.033***	0.032***	0.026***	0.026***
	(0.009)	(0.009)	(0.008)	(0.008)	(0.013)	(0.013)	(0.013)	(0.013)	(0.010)	(0.010)	(0.009)	(0.009)
ΔIT Stock	−0.167***	−0.173***	−0.193***	−0.192***	−0.169***	−0.186***	−0.227***	−0.229***	−0.095	−0.089	−0.083	−0.083
	(0.036)	(0.039)	(0.041)	(0.041)	(0.036)	(0.043)	(0.048)	(0.049)	(0.067)	(0.065)	(0.057)	(0.057)
ΔSER	0.015***				0.023***				0.007			
	(0.005)				(0.007)				(0.007)			
To:												
OECD		0.019***	−0.002			0.028***	0.027**			0.004	0.007	
		(0.007)	(0.008)			(0.009)	(0.012)			(0.010)	(0.010)	
Non-OECD		−0.011				−0.023				0.019		
		(0.020)				(0.026)				(0.033)		
China			0.029***	0.032***			0.031**	0.017			0.054**	0.049**
			(0.008)	(0.011)			(0.014)	(0.015)			(0.025)	(0.022)
India			−0.017***	−0.017***			0.008	0.005			0.026**	0.025**
			(0.004)	(0.004)			(0.007)	(0.006)			(0.010)	(0.009)
ASEAN 6			−0.022	−0.022			−0.046*	−0.036*			−0.019	−0.016
			(0.014)	(0.014)			(0.025)	(0.021)			(0.031)	(0.027)
U.S.				−0.005				0.039**				0.012
				(0.013)				(0.017)				(0.014)
constant	1.144***	1.158***	1.190***	1.198***	1.149***	1.187***	1.209***	1.214***	1.062***	1.041***	0.973***	0.975***
	(0.036)	(0.048)	(0.048)	(0.048)	(0.037)	(0.054)	(0.052)	(0.053)	(0.068)	(0.073)	(0.067)	(0.066)
N	407	407	407	407	244	244	244	244	133	133	133	133
R² (Within)	0.155	0.166	0.269	0.269	0.197	0.215	0.247	0.250	0.143	0.150	0.234	0.235
Adjusted R²	0.382	0.388	0.460	0.460	0.473	0.482	0.498	0.500	0.335	0.334	0.388	0.389
Hausman test	23.88	34.53	31.13	31.68	50.57	40.35	60.64	59.73	2.08	4.86	11.84	11.68
χ^2 (p)	(0.0000)	(0.0000)	(0.0000)	(0.0000)	(0.0000)	(0.0000)	(0.0000)	(0.0000)	(0.5560)	(0.3025)	(0.0656)	(0.0695)

Robust standard errors in parentheses. * $p < 0.10$; ** $p < 0.05$; *** $p < 0.01$. Adjusted R-squared are calculated by least-squares dummy-variables regression. The number of "All industries" does not match the sum of manufacturing and services because "All industries" includes other industries such as primary industries and non-classified industries.

6.4 Discussion

Focusing on the change in the results from the contemporaneous model to the lagged model, several features should be pointed out. First, generally the effect of outsourcing to developing countries turns from negative to non-significant. This indicates that outsourcing to developing countries tends to lower TFP in the first year, but this negative effect disappears in the next year. As stated earlier, the cost effect and the BPR effect are assumed to be realized in a short period of time, but this result shows that any hypothesized effect is not yet realized in the first year. Conversely, the initial cost to arrange outsourcing would have increased the cost share of intermediate inputs, thus lowering TFP. However, in the next year, the cost effect or the BPR effect would compensate the initial cost and the total effect becomes neutral.

Specifically among countries that provide information services, outsourcing to China suggests the clearest effect from negative in the contemporaneous model to positive in the lagged model. Because the positive effect on employment by outsourcing to China is also pointed out in Chapter 5, the benefit of outsourcing to China from Japan is notable in terms of Japanese employment and productivity. This beneficial relationship might be because of the geographical and linguistic proximity as discussed in section 5.1.

On the other hand, the effects of outsourcing to other Asian countries are complicated and not clear. Outsourcing to India is positive in all industries and manufacturing in the contemporaneous model, but it turns negative in all industries and is positive in the service sector in the lagged model. As the amount of offshore outsourcing of information services to India is limited, the effect on India needs continuous assessment to draw implications.

Outsourcing to ASEAN 6 countries causes negative effects in all industries and manufacturing sectors in the contemporaneous model, but these negative effects turn less significant, showing a negative effect only in the manufacturing sector in the lagged model. In general, the initial negative effect on TFP is mitigated with time.

As also seen in Chapter 5, the effect of offshore outsourcing to Asian countries is not homogenous, but rather diverse across countries. Discussing in the lagged model, outsourcing to China suggests the most positive effect both on employment and productivity. On the other hand, outsourcing to ASEAN 6 shows negative effects both on employment and productivity. Outsourcing to India suggests a more complicated effect. It reduces employment, but the effect on productivity depends on the affected industry. Outsourcing to the United States also changes from non-significant to positive, but only in the manufacturing sector. The United States is assumed to provide R&D or cloud computing; therefore, outsourcing of these services would have increased TFP in the manufacturing sector.

In terms of the difference between the manufacturing and service sectors, the manufacturing sector gains positive effects from outsourcing to a wider range of countries. In particular, the manufacturing sector also benefits from outsourcing to high-cost countries such as OECD and the United States. On the other hand, the service sector benefits only from outsourcing to China or India. It is thus possible to infer that the manufacturing sector would take advantage of importing services such as R&D or cloud computing from developed countries.

As pointed out by Jones and Yoon (2008), productivity of the service sector in Japan is far lower than in its manufacturing sector. They argued that this situation is a consequence of the lower levels of competition that result from regulation and less inward FDI in the service sector. As stated earlier, Fukao and Kwon (2006) pointed out that reallocation of resources from less efficient to more efficient firms was very slow and limited in the service sector. These characteristics also might be the reason for a less positive effect of information services outsourcing in the service sector. On the other hand, Minetaki and Nishimura (2010) suggest that outsourcing had a negative impact on the total factor productivity of information services firms in 1990s. However, they mainly discuss domestic outsourcing and assess a contemporaneous effect. Although there are differences in scope and methodology between Minetaki and

Nishimura (2010) and this book, it is inferred that the utilization of IT would affect the economy differently depending on its use on organizational arrangement.

The previous chapter showed that the offshore outsourcing of information services reduces employment in the manufacturing sector in Japan. Increased TFP and reduced employment might be two sides of the same coin. Therefore, in terms of the implications for economic policy, the government should carefully examine how the liquidity of resource reallocation affects employment and TFP. The government also might need to construct statistics to track more comprehensively the volume of outsourcing by specifying trading partners and the objects of trade. Cooperation across countries and global institutions also is desired to obtain more precise statistics and to consider policy measures.

6.5 Conclusion

This chapter provided statistical results on the effect of offshore outsourcing on productivity in Japan with a specific focus on trading partners. As introduced in Chapter 2 in literature review, empirical analyses on the effect of information services outsourcing on productivity is scarce globally. This chapter provided a foundation for future comparative analyses between the U.S., Europe, and Japan.

The results show that the manufacturing sector gains positive effects from outsourcing to high-cost countries such as OECD and the United States as well as the outsourcing to China. On the other hand, the service sector benefits only from outsourcing to China and India. Based on assumptions on the relation between trading partners and outsourced business processes, the manufacturing sector should take advantage of importing services such as R&D and cloud computing from developed countries. In terms of the productivity of the economy, the service sector is becoming a larger component of the economy and the ways to increase productivity in the service sector is one of the major challenges particularly in developed countries. This chapter showed that international trade is affecting productivity not only in the manufacturing sector but also in the services sector.

Discussion in Chapter 3 on organizational view suggests that cloud computing is easier to outsource overseas because of the low level of transaction cost. Therefore, the effect on productivity can be quick and large. However, although the effect on productivity is positive, the effect on employment is negative as shown in Chapter 5. Therefore, empirical results in Chapters 5 and 6 suggest that employment and productivity can have an inverse relation to each other; in other words, typically, offshore outsourcing increases productivity while it reduces employment. As seen in Appendix 5–A, the value added to the Japanese economy as a whole from 2002 to 2006 shows a modest annual growth of 1.6%. Therefore, it can be inferred that offshore outsourcing is not enabling the excessive growth of output, but rather raising productivity while reducing employment. The empirical analysis on the impact on output through the change in employment and productivity is one of the future challenges of this analysis. On the other hand, the relations among output, employment, and productivity are explored from a different angle in the next chapter of this book, using DSGE analysis.

Several limitations and future challenges are associated with this analysis. In addition to the measurement issues mentioned in Chapter 5, other variables such as regulation and R&D also might contribute to the explanations of TFP variations. As mentioned in Chapter 5, comparison with the analysis after 2007 would identify the difference of the effects on the industrial structure before and after the financial crisis, if the data is fully available. Comparative analyses with the U.S., Europe, or Asian countries and firm-based analysis would also be a future challenge.

Chapters 5 and 6 empirically assessed the effect of offshore outsourcing on employment and productivity in 2002–2006. During this period, cloud computing had emerged and was acquiring popularity as a mean of delivering information services. The next chapter specifically focuses on cloud computing, assessing the effect on the economy by a different analytical methodology, a simulation based on the DSGE model.

Appendix 6–A. Summary of statistics

Variable	Observations	Mean	Standard Deviations	Min	Max
ΔTFP	407	1.010	0.044	0.876	1.187
ΔTDO	407	1.061	0.232	0.175	2.522
ΔIT Stock	407	1.019	0.093	0.799	1.361
ΔSER	407	1.194	0.306	0.566	2.067
OECD	407	1.200	0.367	0.513	3.089
Non-OECD	407	1.181	0.331	0.586	3.387
China	407	1.432	0.295	0.720	3.506
India	407	1.307	0.630	0.563	4.906
ASEAN 6	407	1.094	0.416	0.488	3.524
U.S.	407	1.162	0.367	0.517	3.362

Appendix 6–B. Correlations of variables

	ΔTFP	ΔTDO	ΔIT Stock	ΔSER	OECD	Non-OECD	China	India	ASEAN 6	U.S.
ΔTFP	1									
ΔTDO	−0.145***	1								
ΔIT Stock	−0.368***	0.062	1							
ΔSER	−0.260***	0.077	−0.076	1						
OECD	−0.406***	0.117**	−0.034	0.992***	1					
Non-OECD	−0.489***	0.075	0.115**	0.712***	0.767***	1				
China	−0.592***	0.167***	0.127**	0.473***	0.649***	0.833***	1			
India	−0.347***	0.067	0.052	0.751***	0.744***	0.952***	0.771***	1		
ASEAN 6	−0.406***	0.063	0.039	0.796***	0.805***	0.973***	0.772***	0.965***	1	
U.S.	−0.425***	0.131***	0.011	0.854***	0.925***	0.883***	0.822***	0.909***	0.900***	1

* $p < 0.10$; ** $p < 0.05$; *** $p < 0.01$.

CHAPTER 7
Macroeconomic Analysis of Cloud Computing based on the Organizational View

This chapter turns to the "present" stage of the organizational change, which is the adoption of cloud computing. Cloud computing has become one of the major technological changes for business management in the last decade. However, despite the concern about cloud computing's impact on business and the economy, its effect is still not known well. This study constructs a macroeconomic model that incorporates the diffusion of cloud computing by identifying three paths in which cloud computing affects the economy: productivity, entry cost, and sales in the information services sector. The results of impulse response analysis show that the overall effect on the economy is positive assuming a baseline growth of TFP, but is negative without baseline growth. The total effect depends on a combination of productivity growth and the international trade of computing services. The implication of these results is discussed combined with the organizational view shown in Chapter 3 and the empirical results on offshore outsourcing in Chapters 5 and 6.[1]

7.1 Background

Cloud computing has become one of the major topics in information technology architecture. It provides information services from centralized data centers so that firms do not need to invest in and own huge computer resources. General consumers also benefit from cloud computing such as services by Google or Dropbox. However, the business sector has also started to use cloud computing for

---

[1] This chapter is based on Takagi and Tanaka (2014b), which is restructured and revised for this book.

various business services such as information services for email, human resource management, supply chain management, and customer relationship management. For example, Salesforce.com provides a wide range of services such as Customer Relationship Management (CRM).[2] Amazon Web Services also provides a wide range of services such as platforms so that customers can create and provide services on the platform[3].

In terms of the scope of users, cloud computing is categorized as public, private, and hybrid. Public cloud computing is shared by anonymous users globally, and private cloud computing is used by specific user firms or organizations. Hybrid cloud computing combines public and private sources. The present study focuses on aspects of cloud computing such as specialization, outsourcing, and scale benefit; therefore, this study focuses on public cloud computing as the object of study.

These new types of services are rapidly penetrating into the Japanese economy. IPA (2012) shows that the experience of using SaaS (Software as a Service, one of the service models of cloud computing) has grown from 19.5% in 2010 to 33.7% in 2011. The major benefit of cloud computing for customers is cost reduction because firms can share resources with many other customers. Firms can also enjoy flexibility because they can use the computing resources as much as needed without building their own capacity. Because cloud computing is expected to drastically reduce the cost for firms to utilize information technology, it is expected to promote economic growth when a wider range of firms can benefit from IT. On the other hand, cloud computing may be provided from anywhere in the world. If the domestic cloud provider is not competitive, the Japanese economy may face a hollowing-out effect particularly in the information services sector. Therefore, cloud computing has a two-sided potential effect of both growth and challenges.

A number of articles have been published about cloud comput-

---

2   Based on the description at http://www.salesforce.com/products/. Accessed July 4, 2014.
3   Based on the description at http://aws.amazon.com/. Accessed July 4, 2014.

ing, but, as shown in Chapter 2 of this book, the concerns and academic disciplines are scattered across the literature. For example, some studies focus on technological architecture, while others discuss security and privacy. Some studies argue market governance such as competition law and regulation. Despite cloud computing's potential impact on business and the economy, its effect on the economy is not well studied.

From a macroeconomic point of view, analysis with models with a micro-foundation such as the dynamic stochastic general equilibrium (DSGE) model or its foundation, the real business cycle (RBC) model are becoming popular. However, their application is heavily concentrated on financial and monetary policy. DSGE analysis on specific technological innovation and macroeconomic variables is still yet fully utilized.

Therefore, this study tries to construct a model to understand the impact of the diffusion of cloud computing on a macroeconomic scale. This chapter reports the results of impulse response analysis on macroeconomic variables when the economy encounters the diffusion of cloud computing. The model is a prototype for further development, but it also builds a foundation for analysis on a specific technological innovation and its macroeconomic implication.

7.2 Models

The main purpose of this chapter is to implement the impact of cloud computing into macroeconomic models. The base model in which cloud computing is incorporated is the conventional RBC model with monopolistic competition (Griffoli 2010). The base model follows Griffoli (2010) and describes the behavior of households and firms.[4]

---

[4] This analysis used the model of Griffoli (2010) to focus on the extensibility and generality of the model. However, use of a model specifically used for analysis on Japan, such as in Hayashi and Prescott (2002), is a future option.

7.2.1 Base model[5]

This representative household follows the utility function:

$$E_t\sum_{t=0}^{\infty} \beta[logC_t + \psi\log(1 - l_t)] \qquad (7\text{--}1)$$

where C is consumption and l is a unit of labor. Therefore, $1\text{-}l$ represents the time used for leisure. The household maximizes the equation 7–1 under the following budget constraint:

$$c_t + k_{t+1} = w_t l_t + r_t k_t + (1 - \delta)k_t \qquad (7\text{--}2)$$

where k is capital, w is wage, r is the interest rate, and δ is the depreciation rate of capital. $w_t l_t + r_t k_t = y_t$, where y is output under the perfect competition. Note that:

$$i_t = k_{t+1} - (1 - \delta)k_t \qquad (7\text{--}3)$$

where i represents the flow of investment. Therefore,

$$i_t = y_t - c_t \quad . \qquad (7\text{--}4)$$

From the first order condition of 7–1 under budget constraint (7–2), the Euler equation for consumption is obtained as:

$$\frac{1}{c_t} = \beta E_t\left[\frac{1}{c_{t+1}}(1 + r_{t+1} - \delta)\right] \qquad (7\text{--}5)$$

and first order condition for w is:

$$\psi\frac{c_t}{1-l_t} = w_t \quad . \qquad (7\text{--}6)$$

In terms of firm section, each firm i produces output following the Cobb-Douglas function with Harrod-Neutral technological progress:

$$y_{it} = k_{it}^a(e^{zt}l_{it})^{1-a} \qquad (7\text{--}7)$$

where z is the level of technology. Profit of a firm is described as follows:

---

5 Symbols used in the base model are E: expectation, β: discount, ψ: consumption, δ: depreciation, c: consumption, l: labor, k: capital, w: wage, r: interest, y: output, i: investment flow, e^{zt}: productivity.

$$k_{it}^a(e^{zt}l_{it})^{1-a} - w_t l_{it} - r_t k_{it} \qquad (7\text{-}8)$$

Optimal capital labor ratio is obtained from first order conditions for k and l:

$$k: \; ak_{it}^{a-1}(e^{zt}l_{it})^{1-a} = r_t \; . \qquad (7\text{-}9)$$

$$l: \; k_{it}^a(1-a)(e^{zt}l_{it})^{-a} = w_t \; . \qquad (7\text{-}10)$$

Dividing 7–9 by 7–10 yields the optimal capital to labor ratio:

$$k_{it}r_t = \frac{a}{1-a} w_t l_{it} \; . \qquad (7\text{-}11)$$

Under monopolistic competition, price is determined by:

$$p_{it} = \frac{\epsilon}{\epsilon - 1} mc_t p_t \qquad (7\text{-}12)$$

where p_{it} is the firm-specific price, mc_t is marginal cost, and ϵ is the elasticity of substitution. For simplification, individual firms take market price p_t; therefore, $mc_t = (\epsilon-1)/\epsilon$. Combining the marginal cost and the production function, the following conditions are obtained:

$$w_t = (1-a) \frac{y_{it}}{l_{it}} \frac{(\epsilon - 1)}{\epsilon} \; . \qquad (7\text{-}13)$$

$$r_t = a \frac{y_{it}}{k_{it}} \frac{(\epsilon - 1)}{\epsilon} \; . \qquad (7\text{-}14)$$

7.2.2 Implementing cloud computing

In this study, three paths are identified and incorporated into the base model. Before presenting the identification of paths, the diffusion of cloud computing is defined. According to IDC (2012), the share of cloud computing is estimated to be 20% (1 out of 5 dollars spent on software) in 2016. The present study assumes that the origin of commercial cloud computing was around the year 2000, considering Salesforce.com started its business in 1999.[6] Assuming it took 16 years for cloud computing to grow its share to 20%,[7] and

---

6 http://www.salesforce.com/company/#1999 (Accessed on April 2, 2013)
7 This assumption does not suggest that the diffusion rate of cloud computing in Japan necessarily reached 20% in 16 years, but, rather, defines the diffusion path

that marginal diffusion decreased over time, the additional diffusion of cloud computing is defined as follows:

$$cloud_t = \omega cloud_{t-1} + ecloud, \quad 0 < cloud_t < 1 \quad (7\text{–}15)$$

where *ecloud* is white noise with zero means and normal distribution, and in this context, temporary shock starts the diffusion. *cloudt* is defined as the additional penetration rate of cloud computing, which is $0 < cloudt < 1$. The diffusion speed follows the process of an "auto regressive one" (AR(1)) with $\omega=0.95$. To fulfill the assumption that the diffusion reaches 20% in 16 years, *ecloud* is set to 0.018. Based on 7–15, the cumulative diffusion of cloud computing is defined as follows:

$$cum\_cloud_t = \omega_2 cum\_cloud_{t-1} + cloud, \quad 0 < cum\_cloud_t < 1 \quad (7\text{–}16)$$

where $\omega 2=0.999$. As a result, the diffusion of cloud computing follows the path shown in Figure 7–1.

In this analysis, it is assumed that cloud computing affects the economy through three paths. First, cloud computing increases the productivity of firms. Because cloud computing reduces the deployment cost of IT, more firms can enjoy the benefit of IT. The positive effect of IT on productivity has been reported in a significant amount of studies, such as Jorgenson (2002), Jorgenson and Motohashi (2005), and Miyazaki et al. (2012). Overall productivity is supposed to be improved with reduction in the deployment cost of IT. This effect through productivity was discussed in more detail in section 6.3.2.

Second, as seen in prior studies, cloud computing can lower entry costs for new firms, and thus increase the number of new firms. Etro (2009) focuses on this effect and develops a model that depends specifically on the entry cost and the number of firms. Based on this increase in the number of firms, the present study assumes that the

---

shown in Figure 7–1, based on a prior study. Due to the characteristics of DSGE analysis, it is possible to make an analysis at whatever diffusion rate, along with the diffusion paths. Ukai (2013) showed that 10% of Japanese firms which were listed on the Tokyo Stock Exchange had used pure public cloud computing from 2012 to 2013.

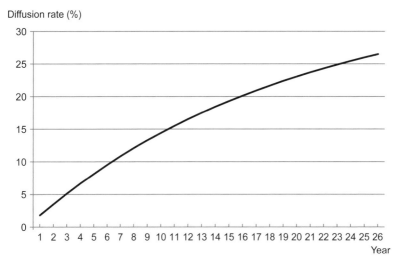

Figure 7-1. Diffusion path of cloud computing

increased number of firms can intensify competition among firms, and thus promote innovation. Newly developed SMEs can also promote innovation and the transfer of employment from the less productive to more productive sector. Therefore, this study assumes that an increased number of firms can raise the productivity of the economy.

Thirdly, cloud computing can reduce the output of the domestic information services industry by intensifying international competition. The key characteristic of cloud computing is the sharing of computing resources among users. The value of service increases as more customers use the same resources, and a wider range of services is provided. As discussed in the analysis about transaction cost economics in Chapter 3, cloud computing requires less proximity to customers; therefore, these network effects can lead competition and monopolistic market structure on a global scale. Global players such as Microsoft, Salesforce, Amazon, and Google are examples of those global players. Cloud computing tends to converge to a smaller number of players on the global scale than traditional IT investment; therefore, the domestic output of information services industry may possibly be reduced by competition with foreign players. In addition to this international competition effect, cloud computing also drastically reduces the cost for using IT by sharing computing resources. This also can reduce the sales of tailor-made information systems; however, this sales may be offset by an increase in the demand for IT as a whole. Therefore, the total expenditure for information services as a whole is not affected in this analysis. Based on these assumptions, these three effects are incorporated into the base model as follows. Productivity level zt is determined by the level of the previous year, by the diffusion of cloud computing, $cloud_t$ and by the number of firms, nt:

$$z_t = \varrho z_{t-1} + \phi cloud_t + \tau n_t \tag{7-17}$$

where ϱ, ϕ and τ are parameters that are calibrated in the next section.

Entry cost η_t is defined as the change ratio from a steady state, and this cost is reduced by the diffusion of cloud computing:

$$\eta_t = \varrho \eta_{t-1} - \theta cloud_t, \quad -1 < \eta_t < 1 \quad . \tag{7-18}$$

In addition, this entry cost can increase the number of firms through:

$$n_t = \gamma \left(n_{t-1} + \chi \frac{vi}{\eta + 1} \right) \tag{7-19}$$

where v is the ratio of investment into new firms among total investment, i. In order to make the entry cost η a non-zero value, entry cost is expressed as $\eta+1$. By adjusting the relative size of new firms and the current number of firms by χ, $\chi\, vi/(\eta+1)$ represents the number of new firms. Following Etro (2009), a certain rate of business is destructed by $1-\gamma$, where γ is set as 0.97.

Finally, subtracting the negative effect of reduced revenue in the information services industry from total output:

$$y_{it} = k_{it}^\alpha (e^{z_t} l_{it})^{1-\alpha} - \mu * cum\_cloud_t \quad . \tag{7-20}$$

Figure 7–2 shows the relations of the endogenous variables. The diffusion of cloud computing affects the variables through the three paths. However, endogenous variables also affect each other. For

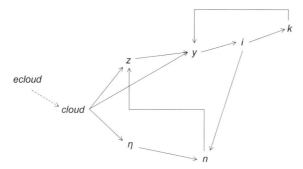

Figure 7–2. Relationship of endogenous variables

example, the number of firms (n) affects productivity (z); capital (k) affects output (y), and investment (i) affects the number of firms (n). Therefore, the diffusion does not simply affect the economy by three paths, but also affects the economy through the intertwined system of variables.[8]

7.2.3 Calibration

In this section, parameters are categorized as structural parameters of the base model and the operational parameters which are used to define the extent of the effects of cloud computing. The structural parameters of the base model are taken from Griffoli (2010) as shown in Table 7–1.[9]

One of the characteristics of the present analysis is that the estimated size of the impact of the diffusion of cloud computing

---

[8] This analysis is based on the stochastic model, which means all variables will return to the original steady state in the very long term (e.g. 100 years). In DSGE analysis, there are options of the stochastic and deterministic models, and the stochastic model assumes the shock is temporary while the deterministic model assumes that the shock is permanent. Considering the productivity effect of information technology, it is also an option to employ the deterministic model; however, it requires identifying new steady state values of all variables. However, the present study focuses on the impact on variables that are not known beforehand. Therefore, this study employs the stochastic model. This is one of the limits of current DSGE analysis.

[9] This study employs the structural parameters of Griffoli (2010) rather than Hayashi and Prescott (2002) or Sugo and Ueda (2008) because the difference of the models would affect applicability of parameters. Incorporating parameters on the Japanese economy by these studies is one of the future challenges for improving the empirical foundation of this book.

Table 7–1. Calibration of structural parameters of the base model

α	β	δ	ψ	ϱ
0.33	0.99	0.023	1.75	0.95

depends on the effects of three paths: productivity, entry cost and the number of firms, and reduced sales. The overall effect on the economy is affected by the combination of the operational parameters that define the impact of these paths. It is relatively possible to make an assumption on the effects of entry cost and reduced sales because of the presence of prior studies and simple structure. However, the effect on productivity is not simple and it is rather controversial. Therefore, operational parameters that define the impact on entry cost and reduced sales are calibrated based on prior studies and a simple assumption, and the parameters that define the effect on productivity are calibrated based on multiple scenarios. Generally, the calibration of operational parameters is conducted by the following procedure. First, the steady state of the base model is calculated before incorporating the diffusion of cloud computing. Each parameter is calibrated so that each of the above-mentioned three paths, through which cloud computing affects macroeconomic variables, has a reasonable impact on the initial steady state values. The impact on entry cost is defined by θ. Etro (2009) estimated that cloud computing can lower entry cost 1% or 5% depending on the speed of diffusion. Using the moderate estimation from Etro (2009), the present study assumes that the entry cost is lowered 1% by the diffusion of cloud computing. Etro (2009) does not specify the penetration rate of cloud computing. For convenience, this study sets the target of diffusion to reach 20% in 16 years from equation 7–15 and Figure 7–1. θ is calibrated so that entry cost (η) is reduced 1% when the cumulative diffusion of cloud computing reaches 20%. Related to the number of firms, χ adjusts the relative size of the total number of firms and newly created firms. According to JSBRI (2012), the latest available percentage of newly created firms among total number of firms is 5.1% from 2004 to 2006. χ is calibrated based on this statistic.

Reduced revenue in the information services industry is defined by μ. Data on the share of foreign cloud services among total cloud services is not available; therefore, this study assumes that half of the services are provided by international providers. If the total spending on IT services does not change, and the diffusion of cloud computing reaches 20%, and the domestic information services industry reduces its output by 10%. As the software and information sharing/providing industry constitutes 4.1% of the GDP of Japan (MIC 2012), the relative size of the impact on total GDP also has to be adjusted. μ is calibrated to fulfill these conditions.

In terms of the effect on productivity, multiple scenarios are assumed, and calibration is conducted based on these scenarios. The growth of total factor productivity (TFP) and its relation to IT investment has received much attention in academic literature, and this issue has been discussed through two main aspects. One aspect is the baseline growth of TFP that is observed even without IT investment, and the other is the impact of IT on TFP that is observed as a contribution of IT investment on TFP growth. Takagi and Tanaka (2012a) show that the average growth rate of TFP between 2002 to 2006 in Japan was approximately 1%, based on a JIP 2009 database. Jorgenson and Motohashi (2003) show that the growth of TFP was 1.13% between 1995 and 2000 including the contribution of IT investment. JSBRI (2008) shows that the average growth of labor productivity between 2000 and 2006 was 2.1%. By taking the moderate assumption, the baseline growth of TFP is assumed to be 1% annually.

However, the effect of IT on TFP is more controversial. Cloud computing promotes the utilization of IT throughout the economy because of the cost reduction effect of using IT. Therefore, the calibration is based on studies of IT investment and productivity. As discussed in Chapter 2, the "productivity paradox" notes that IT investment has not led to a productivity increase since the late 1980s (Solow 1987, Oliner and Sichel 1994, Steiner 1995). However, a positive relation between IT investment and productivity has been gradually reported since the late 1990s, such as in Brynjolfsson and

Hitt (2000).[10] In Japan, positive results have also been reported, although their significance and the size of the impact are diverse across empirical settings and analyzed industrial sectors (e.g. Matsudaira 1998, Takemura 2003). For example, Motohashi (2003) showed that manufacturing companies that utilize information networks achieve 1% higher TFP growth than those without information networks. Considering the diversity in empirical results, the present study assumes the minimum positive effect on productivity by assuming that a 1% increase in the diffusion of cloud computing leads to approximately a 0.01% of productivity (e^z) increase, that is, a 20% diffusion of cloud computing leads to approximately 0.2% productivity growth. Based on these prior studies, ϕ is calibrated following the four scenarios on the productivity effect.

Scenario 1. Both 1% of the baseline growth of TFP and the contribution of cloud computing on TFP are included

Scenario 2. Only 1% of the annual growth of TFP is included, and the contribution of cloud computing on TFP is not included.

Scenario 3. Only the effect of cloud computing is included, and the baseline growth is not included.

Scenario 4. Neither the baseline growth of TFP nor the contribution of cloud computing on TFP is included.

Given the absence of empirical studies, τ, v are set by the following assumptions. τ adjusts the relation between the number of firms and productivity. Therefore, τ is calibrated so that 1% of an increase in the number of firms can lead to approximately 0.01% in the increase of productivity. v sets the ratio of investment in newly created firms among total investment, and it is set to 0.1.

In summary, operational parameters that are used to implement

---

10 In terms of prior studies on IT investment and productivity, see Watanabe and Ukai (2003).

Table 7–2. Calibration of operational parameters

θ	μ	τ	χ	υ
0.07	0.01829	0.0017	1.649	0.1

Table 7–3. Calibration of φ

Scenario 1	Scenario 2	Scenario 3	Scenario 4
1.205	1.195	0.0149	0

the diffusion of cloud computing are calibrated in Tables 7–2 and Table 7–3.[11]

7.3 Results of the Impulse Response Analysis

This section shows the results of impulse response analysis on the four scenarios and the additional analysis.

7.3.1 Results on the productivity effect with four scenarios

Impulse response analysis was conducted on the model with the 0.018 standard error shock on *ecloud* following the diffusion path in Figure 7–1. The results on y (output), z (productivity level), and n (number of firms) are shown in Figure 7–3. The horizontal axis is the period (year), and the vertical axis is the difference from steady state. Note that the movement of variables in the percentages in the following sections refers to the ratio of difference from the steady state. As the present study sets the target of diffusion of cloud computing to reach 20% in the 16th year, the change in GDP, number of firms, and productivity in the 16th year is compared in Table 7–4. The results of the impulse response analysis for all variables are shown in Appendix 7–A, 7–B, 7–C, 7–D, and 7–E, and the steady state values are shown in Appendix 7–F.

As seen in Figure 7–3, the impulse response analysis with scenarios 1 and 2 shows that the most variables move positively by responding to the diffusion of cloud computing. In terms of the effect

---

[11] Productivity grows under $\phi=0$, because an increase in the number of firms contributes TFP to the rise.

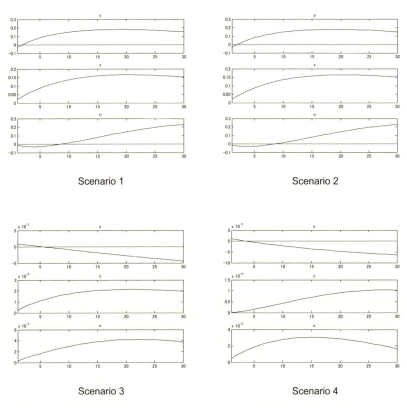

Figure 7–3. Results of the impulse response analysis on *y*, *z*, and *n*

on GDP, a comparison between scenarios 1 and 2 in Table 7–4 shows that a 20% diffusion of cloud computing boosts GDP by 0.2%. Because the GDP of Japan in fiscal year 2012 was 519.6 trillion JPY,[12] 0.2% is translated as 1.04 trillion JPY per year. Without the baseline growth of TFP as in scenarios 3 and 4, GDP decreases.[13] A comparison between scenarios 3 and 4 in Table 7–4 shows that 20% diffusion of cloud computing mitigates the negative effect on GDP by 0.18%.

---

12 Cabinet Office. GDP statistics, http://www.esri.cao.go.jp/jp/sna/menu.html (Accessed on April 9, 2013).
13 An initial increase of *Y* would be because of the increase of investment led by the reduction of entry costs (eta).

Table 7–4. Results at 20% diffusion of cloud computing

	Scenario 1 (Baseline + cloud)	Scenario 2 (Baseline)	Scenario 3 (Cloud)	Scenario 4 (None)	Difference (Scenario 1–2)	Difference (Scenario 3–4)
y (GDP)	18.781%	18.580%	−0.214%	−0.398%	0.20%	0.18%
e^z (Productivity)	17.527%	17.363%	0.207%	0.008%	0.16%	0.20%
n (number of firms)	8.954%	8.859%	0.375%	0.292%	0.09%	0.08%

Difference from steady state.

7.3.2 Analysis on the minimum requirement on TFP

In scenarios 3 and 4, the total effect on GDP becomes negative. In order to explore how much the productivity effect of cloud computing is required to make a total effect positive without baseline growth of TFP, the value of ϕ is adjusted manually. ϕ is required to be at least approximately 0.04 to make the overall results positive. The results of impulse response analysis with ϕ=0.04 is shown in Appendix 7–E. In this setting, GDP grows to its peak at the 9th year to reach 0.143% above its steady state.

ϕ=0.04 means that productivity, which is expressed as e^z, becomes 0.545% above its steady state in the 16th year. This is translated to 0.034% CAGR annual growth of TFP. Under this setting, the productivity increase surpasses the effect of sales reduction in the IT services industry, and makes GDP positive.

7.4 Discussion

The results in the previous section show that a 20% diffusion of cloud computing boosts GDP by 0.18 to 0.2%. However, without the baseline growth of TFP, the total effect on GDP is negative. This means that the sales reduction effect is greater than other positive effects: productivity and an increased number of firms. In order to achieve a positive effect on the economy without baseline growth of TFP, a 20% diffusion of cloud computing needs to raise productivity 0.545%. The present study assumes the minimum positive effect on productivity, assuming a 20% diffusion of cloud computing leads to 0.2% productivity growth. A prior study suggests that firms with information networks achieve a 1% higher TFP (Jorgenson and Motohashi 2003), and the gap between 0.545% and 0.2% is not too large. However, whether it is possible for cloud computing to raise productivity 0.545% is still not certain.

On the other hand, the negative effect is assumed to be caused by the reduction of sales in the information services industry. The present study assumes that the total spending on IT services does not change. However, total spending has continued to grow. Based on data of MIC (2012), the growth rate of the market size of information services sector has been calculated. The result shows that from 2000 to 2010, the information services sector grew by CAGR 4.9%. If this growth continues, the negative effect of reduced sales due to competition with international cloud providers would be mitigated. Additionally, from the practical point of view, the negative effect might be overcome by the baseline growth of TFP as shown in scenarios 1 and 2.

Compared to the prior studies by Etro (2009, 2011), which show that GDP will grow 0.05% to 0.3% as in Table 2–3, the results of the present study suggest that the overall effect depends heavily on the assumption of the impact on each path. The present study suggests a more positive effect on GDP with the baseline growth of TFP, and a more negative effect without baseline growth. It reflects the difference of the model, as the studies of Etro (2009, 2011) specifically depend on business creation and its positive effect, whereas the present study includes multiple paths that include both positive and negative effects.

7.5 Conclusion

This chapter constructs a model to analyze the economic impact of cloud computing. It identifies three paths for cloud computing to affect macroeconomic variables and incorporates them into a standard DSGE framework. Given the practical concerns and the scarcity of prior studies in this field, this chapter fills in a missing part in prior studies. Compared to prior studies by Etro (2009, 2011), the present study proposes a more simplified, yet comprehensive way to understand the effects of the evolution of information technology on the economy.

The results show that a 20% diffusion of cloud computing boosts GDP by 0.18 to 0.2%. However, without a baseline growth of TFP, the total effect on GDP is negative. The possibility to overcome this negative effect is argued against the more positive effect of cloud computing on productivity, the growth of the information services market, and the baseline growth of TFP. From the viewpoints of economic policy, it is important to ensure that the additional use of information technology contributes to the rise of productivity. However, as the analyses in Chapters 5 and 6 showed, the positive relationship between employment and productivity is at least questioned in the results of offshore outsourcing. One of the reasons for the positive relation between productivity and employment in the DSGE analysis in this chapter may be that demand is not fully constrained. If the demand is already fulfilled while productivity rises, the result may be the reduction of inputs. From a practical point of view, it is important to secure employment by the use of information technology while raising productivity.

The discussion in Chapter 3 suggests that cloud computing is relatively easier to outsource overseas because of the low transaction cost. Because the outsourcing of information services could be promoted more if the services are packaged as cloud computing service, it is important to check the development of the contents of the services of cloud computing services globally, and the effects on the economy.

This study contains several challenges for further improvement. First, the model is simple and straightforward, but the size of the impact depends on the calibration of parameters. It might be better for the calibration to be based more on the coverage of the empirical foundations such as cloud computing and entrepreneurship, and cloud computing and the revenue of the information services sector. Alternatively, it would be possible to construct a model in which the variables are determined endogenously and the size of the effects does not depend on calibration. This chapter provides the first step to understanding the technological change and its implications on macroeconomic variables, but this step is ready for further improvement.

Based on the organizational view in part II, quantitative analyses on the impact of organizational change in the forms of offshore outsourcing and cloud computing were conducted in Part III in Chapters 5, 6, and 7. The final part, IV, draws overall implications from these analyses, considering the prospects on the future development of productive organizations.

Appendix 7–A. Impulse response analysis (Scenario 1)

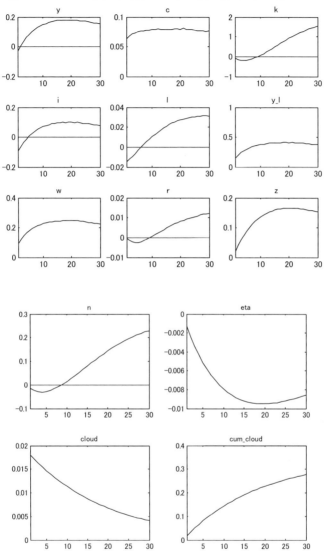

Appendix 7-B. Impulse response analysis (Scenario 2)

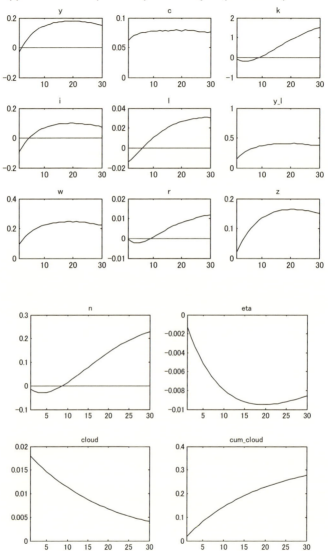

Appendix 7-C. Impulse response analysis (Scenario 3)

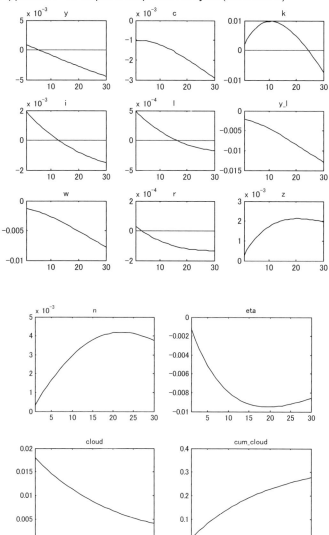

Appendix 7–D. Impulse response analysis (Scenario 4)

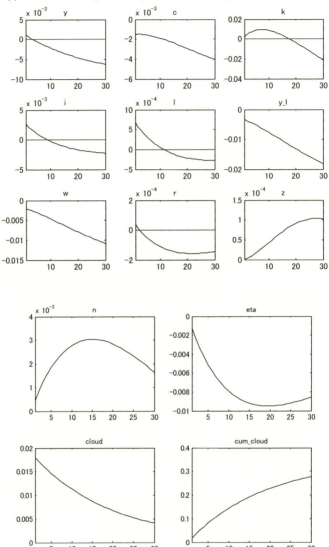

Appendix 7–E. Impulse response with $\varphi = 0.04$

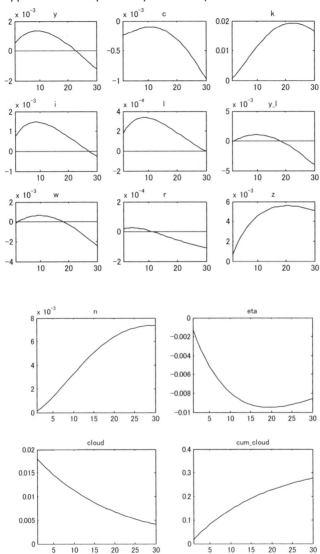

Appendix 7–F. Steady state values

Endogenous variable	Steady state value
y	0.94456
c	0.74963
k	8.47499
i	0.19493
l	0.30273
y_l	3.12011
w	1.88142
r	0.03310
z	0.05716
n	1.03929
eta	0
cloud	0
cum_cloud	0

PART IV
Future Prospects and Conclusion

CHAPTER 8
Mass Collaboration and Open Resources in the Information Age

Previous chapters assessed the impact of offshore outsourcing and cloud computing, which take the organizational form of outsourcings. However, the development of information technology and the Internet not only enabled the outsourcing between organizations but it is also enabling collaboration between smaller units of production, typically individuals. This chapter focuses on the trend of the collaboration of smaller units of production, such as mass "collaboration" and "crowdsourcing," which are stimulated by open data. The aim of this chapter is to describe the phenomena of open data and mass collaboration by illustrating the movement from an organizational economics perspective. This chapter also provides the results of empirical analysis on how the regional characteristics of municipalities affect the decision of local governments to conduct open data initiatives.

8.1 Open Data and Mass Collaboration

Previous chapters assessed how the offshore outsourcing of information services and the utilization of cloud computing affect the Japanese economy. The results indicate that the manufacturing industry raises productivity while reducing employment by offshore outsourcing, and cloud computing increases output and employment if productivity growth is sufficient. Before discussing the interpretation of these results, an important trend, "mass collaboration," associated with outsourcing and industrial structure, is discussed in this chapter.

The arguments of previous chapters are based on transaction cost economics, focusing on the decision whether a business should be conducted in-house or by third-party vendors. Regardless of buying or making, it is assumed that the business is conducted by organizations which contain a significant number of staff and resources. In other words, the previous chapters have dealt with the collaboration between organizations. However, the advancement of information technology and the Internet is not only enabling collaboration between organizations, but it is also enabling collaboration between smaller units of production, such as entrepreneurs, freelance workers, engineers, designers, and amateurs. Tapscott and Williams (2008) describe this trend by the terms "mass collaboration" and "Wikinomics" with examples such as open-source software and an online encyclopedia. "Crowdsourcing" (Howe, 2008) also refers to the participation of individuals into productive activity. This chapter focuses on the trend where the unit of production is becoming smaller and the collaboration between these small units is becoming prominent.

As seen in Chapter 2, most examples in prior studies on mass collaboration are based in North America. On the other hand, Japan-based mass collaboration or crowdsourcing initiatives have not been well reported. However, a new movement, open data, is stimulating the rise of mass collaboration in Japan. Therefore, this chapter focuses on a discussion on mass collaboration in relation to the open data movement in Japan.

Open data is becoming one of the most important phenomena in IT-related fields in Japan. Open data generally refers to a movement in which public organizations provide data which has been held by the organizations in a machine-readable format to the public, so that anyone can reuse the data (Takagi, 2012a). Open data is a world-wide movement which was initially led by the U.S. and UK governments, but is rapidly spreading to many countries in Europe, Asia, and also the Americas. Currently, the open data movement in Japan is emerging with collaboration among small units of production such as individuals. These collaborative activities resemble those labeled "mass collaboration" or "peer production" as well as the communities seen in Open Source Software (OSS). This chapter shares the phenomena of open data and mass collaboration as the object of economic analysis by describing the movement and providing a preliminary analysis. This chapter discusses how open data is associated with mass collaboration from the viewpoint of organizational economics. It also provides the results of empirical analysis on how the regional characteristics of municipalities affect the decision of local governments to conduct open data initiatives.

8.2 Development of Open Data in Japan

In one definition, open data refers to "accessible public data that people, companies, and organizations can use to launch new ventures, analyze patterns and trends, make data-driven decisions, and solve complex problems" (Gurin 2014, p. 9). According to the e-Government Open Data Strategy of Japan, the aims of open data are to (1) Enhance transparency and trust, (2) Promote citizen participation and public-private collaboration, and (3) Vitalize the economy and make public administration efficient.[1] The criteria as open data are different across countries. For example, the U.S. government provides seven principles of open data (OMB 2013). However, the minimum criteria would be those provided by the Ministry of Internal Affairs and Communications (MIC)[2] of Japan, which suggest (1) Provision of data in a machine-readable format and (2) Data with rules allowing the reuse of the data.

Open data is not necessarily limited to governments, but the open data movement has mainly evolved in the public sector (Takagi 2013). To provide data, the U.S. government launched the portal website, "Data.gov" in 2009, and the UK government also launched a similar portal website (Takagi 2012b). Data.gov.uk provides 17,786 data sets and showcases 314 applications related to utilizing

---
[1] IT Strategic Headquarters.: Denshi GyōSei Open Data Senryaku (in Japanese, translated by the author), 2012.
[2] MIC. Open data senryaku no suishin (in Japanese). Translated by the author. http://www.soumu.go.jp/menu_seisaku/ictseisaku/ictriyou/opendata/index.html. Accessed on April 6, 2014.

open data (as of December 2013). In Japan, the national government has started to provide data through Data.go.jp with 9,408 data sets in December 2013. In parallel with the arrangement for data provision, the Open Data Promotion Consortium has been established by the cooperation of private and public organizations to promote open data.

Although open data has various aims, as stated earlier, it is also expected to be a new opportunity for innovation and economic growth. For example, the French government expects that opening up public data will promote the information economy and innovation, and realize growth and employment.[3] The European Commission issued an open data strategy for Europe in December 2011, expecting the economic impact of 40 billion Euros per year for the EU economy (European Commission, 2011). Also, in Japan, the expectation of open data as an economic opportunity has become prominent.[4] Given these expectations, estimation of the economic impact of open data has become a topic of study[5] (Takagi 2012c).

In practice, open data in Japan has advanced from local communities. "Where does my money go?" in a Japanese version[6] originated as an open source web service created by the Open Knowledge Foundation, a non-profit organization in the UK, and is rapidly spreading to local communities in Japan. This service explains public spending in a visual form so that citizens can comprehend the broad view on what amount of public money is spent on what sector. The Japanese version was initially created with data on Yokohama City in 2012, but it is spreading to local communities in Japan, reaching 130 regions as of April 2, 2014. One of the leading

---

3 Council of Ministers on August 31, 2011, http://www.etalab.gouv.fr/article-l-ouverture-des-donnees-publiques-a-l-ordre-du-jour-du-conseil-des-ministres-82988965.html. Accessed on November 25, 2014.

4 For example, a discussion in a governmental committee
http://www.kantei.go.jp/jp/singi/it2/densi/dai2/gijiyousi.pdf (in Japanese). Accessed on November 25, 2014.

5 Vickery, G. "Review of Recent Studies on PSI Re-use and Related Market Developments." http://ec.europa.eu/information_society/newsroom/cf/document.cfm?doc_id=1093. (Accessed November 19, 2014)

6 The web service is available at http://spending.jp/.

regions of open data in Japan is Sabae City in Fukui prefecture, which has published 40 data sets, which are in turn, utilized in 36 applications and tools, as of April 6, 2014.[7] One example is the real-time location data for a community bus which is mapped in the Geographical Information System (GIS), so that residents can identify where the bus is running. On the other hand, Shizuoka prefecture is also providing public data. One of the examples of the reuse is "Fuji-photo", which is a smart phone application to guide users to the best location to take pictures of Mt. Fuji, using location data which is provided by Shizuoka prefecture. In terms of photos of Mt. Fuji, Shizuoka prefecture and Yamanashi prefecture are cooperating together with private organizations to provide a web service to collect digital pictures of Mt. Fuji from users and to provide those pictures as open data.[8]

A number of events such as the "hackathon" or "ideathon" have been organized around the world to explore the opportunity to utilize open data. Hackathon is a one to several days' event through which engineers and designers gather and create new tools. Ideathon is a similar idea-generating event. Usually, the participants of these events are individual engineers, consultants, and experts. The "Where does my money go?" Japanese version has been initially developed at one of these hackathons. "Application contests" are also gaining popularity in Japan. Usually calls for applications last several months, and superior ideas and applications are awarded at the end of the contest period. As one of these utilization events, International Open Data Day is organized by the Open Knowledge Foundation as an annual global event. In 2013, 8 Japanese communities participated among 102 communities worldwide,[9] and in 2014, 32 Japanese communities participated among 111 communities worldwide.[10] Through these events, hundreds of citizens, engineers, consultants, and experts participated in producing

---

7 Sabae City. Data city Sabae. http://www.city.sabae.fukui.jp/pageview.html?id=11552. Accessed on April 6, 2014.
8 http://fugaku3776.okfn.jp/index.php. Accessed on November 23, 2014.
9 http://wiki.opendataday.org/2013/City_Events. Accessed on May 31, 2014.
10 http://wiki.opendataday.org/2014/City_Events. Accessed on May 31, 2014.

value by using open data in Japan. These participants joined the events in each community trying to address various issues by sharing ideas and creating prototypes of solutions.

Open data is also related to the Civic Tech movement which emerged since the early 2010s and refers to the people who participate in creating public value with mainly IT-related skills.[11] A typical example of civic tech is Code for America, a nonprofit organization which hires highly skilled IT engineers and dispatches them to government organizations. More than 60 engineers are dispatched and more than 50 software applications have been developed in various regions (Code for America Website, as of January 2014). The experts who are dispatched to municipalities from Code for America are coders, engineers, and designers who are selected from applicants, and their tasks are diverse and include creating new software, discussing with citizens and public officials how to find and solve issues for a community (Walsh 2013). More than 600 experts applied in 2012, leaving their careers in famous IT firms (Wakabayashi 2013). In Japan, the affiliated organization Code for Japan was launched in 2013. Code for Sapporo, one of the affiliated organization based in Sapporo city, launched a web service to support finding nurseries for parents.[12] This service utilizes data which is provided by various government agencies including Sapporo city. Another case of Civic Tech in Japan is seen in Hack for Japan, which was started mainly by IT engineers just after the Great East Japan Earthquake in March 2011 to help recovery efforts from the disaster.

Open data has various aspects such as government transparency, new business creation, and addressing social issues. However, currently one of the most observable effects is the function of opportunity for the participation and collaboration of individuals.

---

11 Knight Foundation provides a report, "The Emergence of Civic Tech: Investments in a Growing Field," at http://www.knightfoundation.org/media/uploads/publication_pdfs/knight-civic-tech.pdf. Accessed on November 25, 2014.
12 http://www.codeforsapporo.org/papamama/. Accessed on November 25, 2014.

8.3 The Economic Rationality of Mass Collaboration

Why does open data promote the participation and collaboration of individuals? This section discusses how open data leads to mass collaboration from the perspective of organizational economics, as shown in Figure 8–1.

The first element in Figure 8–1 is related to the reduction of entry cost. Open data increases important resources which are freely accessed and used for business. This data can be transformed into various applications and services mainly through the process of software development. In the past, these data were completely unavailable, limited to certain users, or expensive to purchase. Therefore, open data lowers entry cost for entities willing to utilize the data to provide services. Additionally, the development of service platforms, typically provided as cloud computing services, also lowers entry cost. By virtue of these service platforms, anyone can provide smartphone applications or web services to the global market with drastically lower cost. As Etro (2009) empirically showed, cloud computing has the effect of reducing entry cost and promoting business creation. This reduction of entry cost increases the number of smaller entities such as individuals in the market.[13]

The second element is related to the difficulties in searching for the appropriate capability. Economic activity is becoming more and more related to producing intangible products, such as solving social issues, manipulating data, and creating new software and services[14]. However, in activities such as information production, it is not easy to identify the player with a sufficient capability because it

---

[13] This increased number of players is also supported by standardization efforts. Baldwin and Clark (1997) argued that each supplier has freedom and flexibility designing the module as long as the module fits the design rule. Baldwin and Clark (1997) state that "this freedom to experiment with product design is what distinguishes the modular supplier from ordinary subcontractors" (p. 85). In other words, the standardization of modules and the participation of many suppliers have changed the relations of organizations from a command-and-control subcontractor style to collaboration of a larger number of independent entities.

[14] Benkler (2001) relates this shift of economy to organizations, stating that the shift to an economy centered in information and cultural production has enabled non-market and decentralized production.

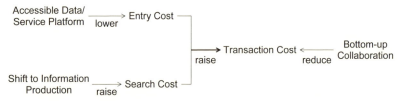

Figure 8–1. Mechanisms for open data to promote mass collaboration

is difficult to foresee the skills and interest of the players, and the quality of products. This difficulty of search is one of the transaction costs of Coase (1937), and important particularly when an increased number of small participants enter the market.[15]

To this point, there is a benefit of bottom-up and collaborative organizations for production. Tapscott and Williams (2008) point out, "When people voluntarily self-select for creative, knowledge-intensive tasks they are more likely than managers to choose tasks for which they are uniquely qualified" (p. 69). This argument is also backed up by organizational economics such as in Garicano and Van Zandt (2013), who suggest that information-processing constraints lead to decentralized decision-making based on different information. Simply put, there is a benefit in leaving decisions on the participation for each player, rather than dispatching the job in a command-and-control organization, because each player knows best about their own capabilities. Bottom-up collaboration in the reuse of open data is rationalized from the increasing number of small, typically independent participants and the information constraint on the capability of information production.

This rationality of collaborative organization is applicable both on open data and OSS. However, currently most initiatives using open data are based on local communities, compared to OSS. For example, in OSS, more than 1,200 engineers are involved in the development of the Linux 3.7 kernel.[16] Other OSSs, such as Apache and Firefox, also aim at being used on a global scale. On the other hand, the major practices of utilizing open data are based more on

---

15 The mediation by information technology such as InnoCentive might have the effect of reducing costs for matching.
16 http://lwn.net/Articles/527191/. Accessed on November 25, 2014.

local interest. This locality also includes situations where most of open data is limited to a certain location, the standardization of the data format is not sufficient, and most of the created software is applicable only to certain data sets. Current use of open data in Japan is characterized by distributed interests, issues, and initiatives which stimulate each other across regions. However, as seen in the global diffusion of the "Where does my money go?" web service, there is the possibility that the use of open data will become more global and scalable.

8.4 Open Data and Regional Characteristics

Whereas open data reuse is mostly limited to local communities, there is a growing expectation of its effects on the vitalization of local communities. However, it would be too early to empirically assess the impact on regional growth. Therefore, instead this section explores the regional characteristics which affect the decision of local governments to conduct open data initiatives. The assessment is conducted by logistic regression analysis as shown in equation 1. The probability of conducting open data initiatives such as creating a portal website and providing public data is defined as $P(y_i)$, where 0 = no conduct, and 1 = the conduct of the open data initiative. i denotes a municipality. It is assumed that the decision is affected by three factors: the log of population (*size*), the rate of population growth (*growth*), and the rate of workers in the ICT sector among all sectors (*ICT*).

$$\text{logit}[P(yi)] = \beta_1 size_i + \beta_2 growth_i + \beta_3 ICT_i. \qquad (8\text{--}1)$$

The list of municipalities which conduct open data initiatives has been taken from Linkdata.org.[17] Other variables have been obtained from the data of the 2010 Population Census, provided by MIC.[18] There might be a gap of time between the census and the

---
17 http://linkdata.org/work/rdf1s127i. Accessed on November 16, 2014. The data is public domain.
18 http://www.e-stat.go.jp/SG1/estat/List.do?bid=000001037709&cycode=0. Accessed on November 25, 2014.

Table 8–1. The results of analysis

	Odds ratio	Standard error	N	Mean	SD	Min	Max
Size	1.842***	0.244	1656	10.182	1.357	6.035	14.796
Growth	0.964	0.046	1656	−3.371	4.929	−19.843	16.354
ICT	1.256*	0.150	1656	1.056	1.137	0.019	7.048

*p<0.10, **p< 0.05, ***p<0.01.

open data initiative, but the 2010 data is used because the explanatory variables generally represent the characteristics of municipalities, and these characteristics are not supposed to change quickly. Among 1,968 municipalities including wards, 66 municipalities are conducting open data initiatives. In order to control the size and the role of local government, the data of prefectures and wards in cities are excluded. The outlier is eliminated once from the dataset by the standard that values are within the means plus/minus four times standard deviations. As a result, 51 municipalities are conducting open data initiatives among 1,656 municipalities. The summary of statistics and the results of the logistic regression analysis are shown in Table 8–1.[19]

As seen in the results, the size of the municipality and the ratio of workers in the ICT sector were found as positive determinants on the local governments' choices on open data initiatives. It would be reasonable to suppose that new initiatives such as open data are tried by large municipalities that have sufficient resources. However, relatively small towns in Fukui prefecture are also conducting open data by cooperating with other municipalities in the prefecture. In this sense, it is inferred that a significant result on the scale of the municipality is not a prerequisite for conducting the open data initiative. On the other hand, the ratio of ICT workers would be more important because open data requires residents who can utilize and create value from the data.

---

19 Analysis is conducted using STATA/IC 11.2. Hosmer-Lemeshow χ^2=3.20, p=0.9213. Multicollinearity is not detected, but correlation between explanatory variables is observed. Handling of multicollinearity and the improvement of the selection of explanatory variables are future challenges.

8.5 Implications and Future Challenges

As seen in Section 3, the current development of open data in Japan is characterized by its use in the local community. It is meaningful that open data contributes to local development, but in order to promote the expected economic growth, scalability is one of the important elements in promoting open data policy. If data is limited to a certain region, created software or services are used only by a small number of users, which would reduce the incentives for engineers to use the data. Conversely, if an application is used universally, there would be an opportunity to collect the knowledge needed to improve the application, as seen in OSS. Therefore, policies to ensure the scalability of data, such as standardization of data and centralized or integrated data collection, are encouraged. On the other hand, the results of empirical analysis in Section 4 suggest that it would be important to see if there are sufficient people who use the data. If there are sufficient users in a community, it will be easier for local governments to start open data initiatives.

Open data in Japan is emerging with the trend of mass collaboration. Compared to collaboration between established organizations such as outsourcing, it is difficult to capture the activity of individuals and measure their impact on the national economy. Additionally, the reuse of data typically involves creating information services, whose value is not necessarily related to the quantity of output.

This indirect relation of output and value has also been related to the intrinsic nature of information. Noguchi (1974) pointed out that the value of information can be measured by the reduction of uncertainty, but this value is not related to the quantity of information[20] and, moreover, the value and price of information is a different concept because the value is determined by the demand side whereas the price is determined by the combination of demand and

---

[20] He suggests that program information can be assessed as productivity, and information for consumption can be assessed as certain units of quantity, such as time and the number of letters.

supply. On the other hand, Bressand (1991) also suggested that the value of information has to be realized by the cooperation of a producer and consumer, and the price of information is attached to the relationship between them, rather than the object of trade. In either case, the value of information cannot be measured or realized without depending on a certain customer. Mass collaboration is still not a major component of the economy. However, traditional approaches of economics focusing on output and productivity may face questions when the economy is more information-centered, and the relation between output, value, and income becomes more indirect.

This section discussed the "future" stage of the framework presented in Chapter 1, by discussing mass collaboration based on a description of the latest practices and a qualitative argument. While previous chapters focused on outsourcing relations between organizations, this section discussed how the development of IT has enabled not only collaboration between organizations, but also between individuals. Mass collaboration is still in its initial stages particularly in Japan, and it is still not clear if it will become one of the major forms of production. However, as seen in this section, mass collaboration and outsourcing partly share common ground in terms of the development of IT and transaction costs. As discussed in Chapter 1, organizational structure is continuously affected by the development of IT. Therefore, it is worthwhile to take into account the future development of organizational structure to discuss the implications from the analyses in Chapters 4 to 7. The next section integrates the results of the analyses on offshore outsourcing and cloud computing in previous chapters and also the argument on mass collaboration, to discuss overall implications throughout this book.

8.6 Conclusion

This chapter focused on the "future" stage, discussing mass collaboration based on a description of the latest practices and a qualitative argument. While previous chapters focused on outsourcing relations between organizations, this chapter discussed the collaboration of smaller entities enabled by environmental changes such as open data. This chapter described the latest movement of open data and civic tech not covered in prior studies on mass collaboration, and also discussed how open data enables mass collaboration. Collaboration of smaller entities was beyond the initial framework on organizational structure in Chapter 3; therefore, the discussion of economic rationality on mass collaboration in this chapter is an extension of the initial framework of organizational structure found in Chapter 3.

The description on open data and civic tech suggests that there is a new environment for economic activities, such as open resources and smaller entities for production. Although these movements are still in the initial stage, they show the trend that individuals are engaging in the production of social value more autonomously with certain skills. This chapter also showed the economic rationality of mass collaboration by transaction cost economics. It suggested that mass collaboration is the extension of outsourcing from the viewpoint of transaction cost economics. Additionally, the emergence of mass collaboration is discussed with the shift to an information-centric economy. The discussion suggested that the traditional economics approach may face challenges when the economy becomes more information-centric, due to the difficulty to capture economic impact and indirect relations between output and value.

The final chapter integrates the results of quantitative analysis on offshore outsourcing and cloud computing in previous chapters and the qualitative argument on mass collaboration in this chapter. It draws overarching implications from the above analyses on past, present, and future stages.

CHAPTER 9
Conclusion

9.1 Key Findings of the Analyses

This book analyzed the impact of information technology on the economy, through structural change in productive organizations, following the stages from the past to present. Chapter 3 discussed the underlying perception of organizational structure, specifically the mechanisms behind a firm's decisions on the outsourcing of information services using transaction cost economics and service attributes. In particular, the discussion showed that the development of information technology affects service attributes such as heterogeneity and simultaneous production and consumption, which in turn affect transaction costs, such as opportunism and bounded rationality. Chapter 3 also provided the framework and the analytical tool to operationalize the theory to better understand a firm's choices of organizational structure. Discussion on organizational structure in Chapter 3 suggests that the development of IT affects the structure of productive organizations to a more decentralized and disintegrated form, through standardization and the development of communication networks. Based on these arguments on organizational structure, quantitative analyses were conducted with organizational change from past to present.

Chapter 4 provided an analysis on national culture as a key determinant for FDI inflow, with a comparison of the different impact in service and non-service sectors. By using the AsiaBarometer to represent national culture, this chapter confirmed that national culture influences FDI inflow in service sector, and that a specifically strong pride of one's own country and conservativeness have a negative effect on service FDI inflow, whereas they have no significant effect on non-service FDI inflow in developing Asian countries. As part of the service sector, the location of information services should also be affected by cultural characteristics, although the effect might be mitigated by the standardization effect.

In the "past" stage, analyses on the impact of offshore outsourcing of information services in Chapters 5 and 6 showed that offshore outsourcing can generally raise productivity while reducing employment. From these analyses, it can be inferred that the outsourcing of high value-added services to high-cost countries can reduce employment while raising productivity, particularly on the manufacturing sector. On the other hand, the analyses revealed that the results are not uniform across trading partners. In particular, it was found that there are diverse effects depending on the trading partners, even across Asian countries.

In the "present" stage, DSGE analysis on cloud computing in Chapter 7 suggested that the key to achieving positive results from the utilization of cloud computing is productivity growth and a balance of international trade in computing services. However, as discussed in Chapter 7, a positive relationship between productivity and employment is not guaranteed. Particularly when demand is insufficient, a positive effect of productivity on employment is in question. As the discussion on organizational structure and transaction cost in Chapter 3 suggests, cloud computing can be easily outsourced even overseas because of the low transaction cost. Additionally, the outsourcing of computing resources is less visible to society than the outsourcing of traditional information services because it is the outsourcing of a common layer across multiple business functions rather than the outsourcing of a whole business unit such as call-center operation or software development. In this sense, the impact can become large and quick.

For the "future" stage, mass collaboration which is stimulated by open data was discussed. Chapter 8 described the latest movement of open data and civic tech which was not covered in prior studies on mass collaboration, and also discussed how open data enables mass collaboration. Collaboration of smaller entities is beyond the initial framework on organizational structure in Chapter 3; therefore, the discussion on economic rationality on mass collaboration in this chapter is the extension of the initial framework of organizational structure in Chapter 3. Description on open data and civic tech suggests that there is a new environment for economic activities, such as open resources and smaller entities for production. Although these movements are still in the initial stage, they show a trend where individuals are engaging in the production of social value more autonomously with certain skills. This chapter also suggested that mass collaboration is the extension of outsourcing from the viewpoint of transaction cost economics. Additionally, the emergence of mass collaboration is discussed with the shift to an information-centric economy. The discussion suggested that the traditional economics approach may face challenges when the economy becomes more information centric, due to the difficulty to capture economic impact and indirect relations between output and value.

Based on the findings and arguments in these preceding chapters, the overall implications are discussed in the next section.

9.2 Overall Implications

As discussed in Chapter 1, this research has advanced the discussion on the economic impact of IT by providing an integrated view on the organizational changes which are brought about by the development of information technology. Based on the argument in Chapter 3 about how information technology has affected organizational structure, the economic impacts of offshore outsourcing of information services are assessed in Chapters 5 and 6. On the other hand, Chapter 6 analyzed the economic impact of cloud computing. In addition, the previous section in this chapter has discussed mass collaboration, combined with the latest movement of open data and the shift to an information-centric economy.

Each analysis has complex findings which are discussed in each chapter. This section integrates these findings and draws key implications which are obtained throughout the analyses based on the integrated approach of this research. The key implications can be summarized into three points as follows.

- **Organizations are changing to a vertically disintegrated form through the development of IT**

As seen in Chapter 3, the development of information technology reduces service attributes such as heterogeneity and simultaneous production and the consumption of information services. This reduction of service attributes lowers a part of transaction costs, such as the risk of opportunism and uncertainty. In particular, the development of communication networks and tools has played an important role in reducing uncertainty when the services are conducted in distant locations, and the standardization of services associated with the development of tools including CRM reduced the risk of opportunism. Cloud computing is an advanced form of taking advantage of standardization and improved communication networks.

These technological developments are also the results of social and business demand. Offshore outsourcing of information services is driven by the demand of businesses that try to benefit from a difference in factor prices, such as wages, land, and energy. On the other hand, cloud computing is promoted by the expectation of computing services on the scale economy, by both providers and customers. In this context, technological development has realized the feasibility of meeting these business demands on the economy of scale. As a result, hierarchical, vertically integrated organizations are able to separate certain information services and outsource them to third-party vendors. In the last decade, this took the form of offshore outsourcing and cloud computing suggesting the trend to vertical disintegration of organizations.

With the rise of the possibility to standardize business processes, outsourced information services are facing an opportunity to be accumulated globally to enjoy the merits of the scale economy by serving more customers worldwide. This is particularly observed in the form of cloud computing, and suggests the trend to horizontal accumulation. Therefore, the impact of IT suggests a trend in the rearrangement of business functions along with the direction to vertical disintegration, and possibly horizontal accumulation.

However, the trend of mass collaboration suggests that there is an area in which it is difficult to benefit from the scale economy. This is because of the heterogeneous nature of the contents of the information and required activities, from finding the issues in a community to creating tailor-made applications. In a sense, mass collaboration fills in the area which needs variety in knowledge and information, and cannot be addressed by organizations which aim at a scale economy.

- **Overcoming downward pressure on employment is the key to benefiting from IT**

The assessment on the impact of offshore outsourcing on the economy in Chapters 4 and 5 suggested that downward pressure on employment is generally prominent in Japan. In particular, these analyses showed that the impact of offshore outsourcing is on the rise in productivity and in the reduction of employment. On the other hand, the DSGE analysis on cloud computing in Chapter 6 suggested that it is also possible to raise output and employment, if productivity growth is sufficient.

However, as discussed in Chapter 7, one of the reasons for the positive relation between productivity and employment in the DSGE analysis may be the unconstrained demand. In this sense, in order to realize the benefit of IT on the economy, it is important to ensure that IT contributes to the development of new products or services which create new demand.

Additionally, this research assumes that organizational changes evolve along a timeline, but this evolution does not necessarily mean these organizations shift one after another exclusively. Instead, these new organizational forms can evolve and overlap each other; therefore, offshore outsourcing and cloud computing can be utilized simultaneously. Additionally, as discussed in Chapter 1, the evolution of organizational structure can accelerate with the accumulation of available technologies. In this sense, the impact of IT on the economy depends on how comprehensively the results are taken into consideration. From the analyses in this book, it is inferred that IT contributes to productivity growth through offshore outsourcing, but is not sufficient to support the growth of the whole economy. Instead, ensuring that information technology creates new demand is important in making the economy sustainable, particularly in terms of employment.

- **There are significant differences among Asian countries as trading partners.**

One of the other findings in this research is that the effect of offshore outsourcing on the economy depends on the trading partner, even within Asian countries. In terms of the effect on employment in the lagged model in Chapter 4, only outsourcing to China has a positive effect on manufacturing employment, whereas outsourcing to India and the ASEAN 6 countries has negative effects. In terms of the effect on productivity in the lagged model in Chapter 5, outsourcing to China has a positive effect, whereas outsourcing to ASEAN 6 countries has a negative effect.

The most highlighted result is the uniqueness of China as a trading partner of Japan. Outsourcing to China has a positive effect both on employment and productivity in the lagged model. As introduced in Chapter 5, China has the unique characteristic of linguistic proximity with Japan. There has also been an established relation between China and Japan as trading partners.[1] The linguistic proximity and experience as trading partners should contribute to achieving positive effects from information services outsourcing to China.[2]

In the argument about economic integration in Asia, Fujita

---

[1] Fujita (2007a) suggests that China was the second largest export-partner and the top import-partner of Japan in 2004.
[2] In addition, Takagi (2011) shows that cultural characteristics are important factors

(2007b, p. 5), for example, discussed that the intra-trade share of East Asia[3] has been increasing rapidly, from 34.9% in 1980 to 52.4% in 2003. These arguments on economic integration emphasize the interdependency of the economy in certain regions across countries. However, this book showed that there is significant diversity in the effects of the international trade of information services on the national economy depending on trading partners. In this sense, it is important to consider how to realize mutually beneficial relationships with each country, instead of generalizing Asia as a trading partner.

9.3 Academic Implications

In contrast to prior studies which directly assessed the relations between information technology and productivity, this book has taken organizational changes into consideration as intermediaries to connect IT and economic impact. By doing so, this book has shed light inside the mechanisms by which IT affects the economy.

This book also discussed statistical evidence on the impact of the offshore outsourcing of information services from Japan by specifying trading partners. In particular, the book showed the variety in the effects of offshore outsourcing. These results suggest the importance of examining the effects of trade with Asian countries in detail, rather than generalizing Asia as a trading partner.

On the other hand, Chapter 7 has particularly advanced a way to use the DSGE approach flexibly to a wider range of topics including the impact of information technology. Compared to prior studies, this study provided a more flexible and comprehensive model to analyze technological development and its impact on economic variables. On the other hand, the argument in the final chapter suggested the challenges of the traditional approach of economic

---

    in drawing foreign direct investment into the service sector. Takagi (2011) does not discuss the proximity between trading partners, but suggests the importance of intangible factors such as culture and language in the service sector.

3 East Asia in this analysis in Fujita (2007b) consists of the ASEAN 10, China, Japan, Hong Kong, South Korea, and Taiwan.

analyses, including the DSGE approach, when the economy consists more of activities on information production.

Each chapter provided new findings and discussions on each topic, and this book as a whole has integrated the discussions on each topic to draw implications on the impact of information technology on the economy through organizational changes. In particular, this book integrated multiple organizational changes in an evolutionary path, which is explained by transaction cost economics. This book also showed a way to assess the economic impact of information technology along with the evolutionary path, integrating macro and microeconomic approaches. This integrated approach is also a contribution of this book.

9.4 Future Challenges in an Age of Networked Production

Challenges for the future regard geographical aspects in an age of networked production. The web of production, which consists of individuals around the world, is becoming observable. On the other hand, a geographical perspective is still important in terms of infrastructures, environment, quality of life, and availability of products and variety of services. These factors are also important for creative work such as discussed by Florida (2007). Therefore, a future challenge is to build a general theory on the geographical aspects of a production network, applicable in the age of networked and mass collaboration. This challenge should include a discussion on the capability of creative works and their agglomeration, the relation of a community to build global production networks, and changes in the locational constraints in productive activities in a global production network.

The second challenge for the future is how to incorporate the value of information in current economic frameworks, such as in production functions. The value of information might be accumulated somewhere instead of the site of production. This difficulty in capturing the value of information suggests other challenges for the current economic framework.

The third challenge for the future is quantifying the impact of IT on organizational structure. Measuring the transaction costs in information services and analyze how much these costs are reduced by the development of IT is important for future understanding of IT on organizational structure. The approach of quantifying the transaction costs also includes identifying the threshold of transaction costs by which firms decide to outsource the business process to outside entities within or outside of a country.

Rapid development of IT is still ongoing and its effect on society is also continuing. Thus the central issue in future challenges is finding a balance between the inclusion of the latest developments and building a general theory which can be applied throughout a wide variation of phenomena.

References

Amiti, Mary and Shang-Jin Wei. 2005. "Fear of Service Outsourcing: Is it Justified?" *Economic Policy* 42: 307–339.

———. 2009. "Service Offshoring and Productivity: Evidence from the US." *World Economy* 32, no. 2: 203–220. Accessed April 22, 2014. doi:10.1111/j.1467-9701.2008.01149.x.

Anderton, Bob and Paul Brenton. 1999. "Outsourcing and Low-Skilled Workers in the UK." *Bulletin of Economic Research* 51, no. 4: 267–285.

Ang, Soon and Detmar W. Straub. 1998. "Production and Transaction Economies and IS Outsourcing: A Study of the U.S. Banking Industry." *MIS Quarterly* 22, no. 4: 535–552.

Anthes, Gary. 2010. "Security in the Cloud." *Communications of the ACM* 53, no. 11: 16–18. Accessed July 23, 2012. doi:10.1145/1839676.1839683.

Aoki, Masahiko and Haruhiko Ando. 2002. *Module-Ka: Atarashii Sangyō Architecture no Honshitsu* (in Japanese). Tokyo: Toyo Keizai Shinpō-sha.

Arndt, Sven W. 1998. "Super-Specialization and the Gains from Trade." *Contemporary Economic Policy* 16, no. 4: 480–485.

Arthur, W. Brian. 2009. *The Nature of Technology*. Free Press.

Bahli, Bouchaib and Suzanne Rivard. 2003. "The Information Technology Outsourcing Risk: A Transaction Cost and Agency Theory-Based Perspective." *Journal of Information Technology.* 18, no. 3: 211–221.

Baldia, Sonia. 2007. "Intellectual Property in Global Sourcing: The Art of the Transfer." *Georgetown Journal of International Law* 38, no. 3: 499–528.

Baldwin, Carliss Y. and Kim B. Clark. 1997. "Managing in an Age of Modularity." *Harvard Business Review* 75, no. 5: 84–93.

———. 2000. *Design Rules: The Power of Modularity*. Cambridge, Ma.: MIT Press.

Baldwin, Richard and Frederic Robert-Nicoud. 2007. "Offshoring: General Equilibrium Effects on Wages, Production and Trade." *NBER Working Papers*: 12991. Accessed June 29, 2014. http://www.nber.org/papers/w12991.pdf.

Bartel, Ann, Saul Lach, and Nachum Sicherman. 2005. "Outsourcing and Technological Change." *NBER Working Papers*: 11158. Accessed June 29, 2014. http://www.nber.org/papers/w11158.pdf.

Bayrak, Ergin, John P. Conley, and Simon Wilkie. 2011. "The Economics of Cloud Computing." Working Paper No. 11-W18. Department of Economics, Vanderbilt University.

BEA. 2011. *U.S. International Services: Cross-Border Trade 1986–2008, and Services Supplied through Affiliates, 1986–2007,* United States Bureau of Economic Analysis. Accessed July 10, 2011. http://www.bea.gov/international/intlserv.htm.

Benkler, Yochai. 2007. *The Wealth of Networks: How Social Production Transforms Markets and Freedom*. Yale University Press.

Berman, Eli, John Bound, and Zvi Griliches. 1994. "Changes in the Demand for Skilled Labor within U.S. Manufacturing: Evidence from the Annual Survey of Manufactures." *Quarterly Journal of Economics* 109, no. 2: 367–397.

Bienstock, Carol C. and John T. Mentzer. 1999. "An Experimental Investigation of the Outsourcing Decision for Motor Carrier Transportation." *Transportation Journal* 39, no. 1: 42–59.

Bills, Scott. "Standardization and Simplification – the Keys to Unlocking Cloud Value." Accessed April 22, 2014. http://leverhawk.com/simplification-and-standardization-the-keys-to-unlocking-cloud-value-20130209196.

Black, Sandra E. and Lisa M. Lynch. 2004. "What's Driving the New Economy?: The Benefits of Workplace Innovation." *Economic Journal* 114, no. 493: F97–F116. Accessed March 12, 2014. doi:10.1111/j.0013-0133.2004.00189.x.

Blair, Margaret M., Erin O'Hara O'Connor, and Gregg Kirchhoefer. 2011. "Outsourcing, Modularity, and the Theory of the Firm." *Brigham Young University Law Review* 2011, no. 2: 263–314.

Botsman, Rachel and Roo Rogers. 2011. *What's Mine is Yours: The Rise of Collaborative Consumption*. Collins.

Brabham, Daren C. 2012. "The Myth of Amateur Crowds." *Information, Communication & Society* 15, no. 3: 394–410. Accessed January 5, 2014. doi:10.1080/1369118X.2011.641991.

Bresnahan, Timothy and Jonathan Levin. 2013. "Vertical Integration and Market Structure." In *Handbook of Organizational Economics*, edited by Robert Gibbons and John Roberts, 853–890: Princeton University Press.

Bresnahan, Timothy F., Erik Brynjolfsson, and Lorin M. Hitt. 2002. "Information Technology, Workplace Organization, and the Demand for Skilled Labor: Firm-Level Evidence." *Quarterly Journal of Economics* 117, no. 1: 339–376. Accessed March 12, 2014. doi:10.1162/003355302753399526.

Bressand, Albert. edit. 1991. *Networld*. (in Japanese) Toyo Keizai Shinpō-Sha.

Brynjolfsson, Erik. 1993. "The Productivity Paradox of Information Technology." *Communications of the ACM* 36 (12): 67–77.

Brynjolfsson, Erik and Lorin Hitt. 1996. "Paradox Lost? Firm-Level Evidence on the Returns to Information Systems Spending." *Management Science* 42, no. 4: 541–558.

———. 2000. "Beyond Computation: Information Technology, Organizational Transformation and Business Performance." *Journal of Economic Perspectives* 14, no. 4: 23–48. Accessed April 22, 2014. doi:10.1111/j.1468-0297.2010.02384.x.

Brynjolfsson, Erik, Thomas W. Malone, Vijay Gurbaxani, and Ajit Kambil. 1994. "Does Information Technology Lead to Smaller Firms?" *Management Science* 40, no. 12: 1628–1644.

Budhathoki, Nama R. and Caroline Haythornthwaite. 2013. "Motivation for

Open Collaboration: Crowd and Community Models and the Case of OpenStreetMap." *American Behavioral Scientist* 57, no. 5: 548–575. Accessed January 5, 2014. doi:10.1177/0002764212469364.

Chen, Yongmin, Ignatius J. Horstmann, and James R. Markusen. 2008. "Physical Capital, Knowledge Capital and the Choice between FDI and Outsourcing." *NBER Working Papers*: 14515. Accessed June 29, 2014. http://www.nber.org/papers/w14515.pdf.

Coase, Ronald H. 1937. "The Nature of the Firm." *Economica* 4, no. 16: 386–405.

———. 1988. *The Firm, the Market, and the Law*. Chicago: University of Chicago Press.

Cretu, Liviu-Gabriel. 2012. "Cloud-Based Virtual Organization Engineering." *Informatica Economica* 16, no. 1: 98–109.

Cudanov, Miaden, Jovan Krivokapic, and Jovan Krunic. 2011. "The Influence of Cloud Computing Concept on Organizational Performance and Structure." *Management* 60: 18–25.

Cusumano, Michael A. 2010. *Staying Power: Six Enduring Principles for Managing Strategy & Innovation in an Uncertain World*. Oxford University Press.

Dhawan, Rajeev, Karsten Jeske, and Pedro Silos. 2008. "Productivity, Energy Prices, and the Great Moderation: A New Link." *Federal Reserve Bank of Atlanta Working Paper* 2008–11: 1–14.

Dibbern, Jens, Jessica Winkler, and Armin Heinzl. 2008. "Explaining Variations in Client Extra Costs between Software Projects Offshored to India." *MIS Quarterly* 32, no. 2: 333–366.

Dodge, Martin and Rob Kitchin. 2013. "Crowdsourced Cartography: Mapping Experience and Knowledge." *Environment & Planning A* 45, no. 1: 19–36. Accessed January 5, 2014. doi:10.1068/a44484.

Durkee, Dave. 2010. "Why Cloud Computing Will Never be Free." *Communications of the ACM* 53, no. 5: 62–69.

Endo, Patricia Takako, Andre Vitor de Almeida Palhares, Nadilma Nunes Pereira, Glauco Estacio Concalves, Djamel Sadok, Judith Kelner, Bob Melander, and Jan-Erik Mangs. 2011. "Resource Allocation for Distributed Cloud: Concepts and Research Challenges." *IEEE Network* 25, no. 4: 42–46. Accessed July 23, 2012. doi:10.1109/MNET.2011.5958007.

Estellés-Arolas, Enrique and Fernando González-Ladrón-de-Guevara. 2012. "Towards an Integrated Crowdsourcing Definition." *Journal of Information Science* 38, no. 2: 189–200. Accessed January 5, 2014. doi:10.1177/0165551512437638.

Etro, Federico. 2009. "The Economic Impact of Cloud Computing on Business Creation, Employment and Output in Europe: An Application of the Endogenous Market Structures Approach to a GPT Innovation." *Review of Business and Economics* 54, no. 2: 179–208.

———. 2011. "The Economics of Cloud Computing." *IUP Journal of Man-

agerial Economics 9, no. 2: 7–22.
European Commission. 2011. *Press Release, Digital Agenda: Turning Government Data into Gold*, Accessed April 6, 2014. http://europa.eu/rapid/press-release_IP-11-1524_en.htm.
Falk, Martin and Yvonne Wolfmayr. 2008. "Services and Materials Outsourcing to Low-Wage Countries and Employment: Empirical Evidence from EU Countries." *Structural Change & Economic Dynamics* 19, no. 1: 38–52. Accessed April 22, 2014. doi:10.1016/j.strueco.2007.12.001.
Feenstra, Robert C. and Gordon H. Hanson. 1997. "Foreign Direct Investment and Relative Wages: Evidence from Mexico's Maquiladoras." *Journal of International Economics* 42: 371–393.
———. 1999. "The Impact of Outsourcing and High-Technology Capital on Wage Estimates for the United States." *Quarterly Journal of Economics* 114, no. 3: 907–940.
———. 2003. "Global Production Sharing and Rising Inequality: A Survey of Trade and Wages." In *Handbook of International Trade*, edited by E. Kwan Choi and James Harrigan, 146–185. Blackwell Publishing.
Florida, Richard. 2007. *The Flight of the Creative Class: The New Global Competition for Talent*. Harper Business.
Ford, Emily. 2013. "Defining and Characterizing Open Peer Review: A Review of the Literature." *Journal of Scholarly Publishing* 44, no. 4: 311–326. Accessed January 5, 2014. doi:10.3138/jsp.44-4-001.
Frankrone, Erin R. 2013. "Free Agents: Should Crowdsourcing Lead to Agency Liability for Firms?" *Vanderbilt Journal of Entertainment & Technology Law* 15, no. 4: 883–912.
Fujita Masahisa. 2007a. Development of East Asian regional economies: A view from spatial economics. In *Regional Integration in East Asia – From the Viewpoint of Spatial Economic*, edited by Masahisa Fujita. 64–90. IDE-JETRO.
———. 2007b. Globalization, regional integration and spatial economics: An introduction. In *Regional Integration in East Asia - From the Viewpoint of Spatial Economic*, edited by Masahisa Fujita. 1–22. IDE-JETRO.
Fukao, Kyoji and Hyeog Ug Kwon. 2006. "Why did Japan's TFP Growth Slow Down in the Lost Decade? An Empirical Analysis Based on Firm-Level Data of Manufacturing Firms." *Japanese Economic Review* 57, no. 2: 195–228. Accessed April 22, 2014. doi:10.1111/j.1468-5876.2006.00359.x.
Garicano, Luis and Timothy Van Zandt. 2013. "Hierarchies and the Division of Labor." In *Handbook of Organizational Economics*, edited by Robert Gibbons and John Roberts, 604–654: Princeton University Press.
Gibbons, Robert and John Roberts. 2013. "Introduction." In *Handbook of Organizational Economics*, edited by Robert Gibbons and John Roberts, 1–10: Princeton University Press.
Goodchild, Michael F. and J. Alan Glennon. 2010. "Crowdsourcing Geo-

graphic Information for Disaster Response: A Research Frontier." *International Journal of Digital Earth* 3, no. 3: 231–241. Accessed January 5, 2014. doi:10.1080/17538941003759255.

Gottfredson, Mark, Rudy Puryear, and Stephen Phillips. 2005. "Strategic Sourcing-from Periphery to the Core." *Harvard Business Review*, February 2005.

Gratton, Lynda. 2011. *The Shift: The Future of Work is Already here.* Harper-Collins Business.

Griffoli, Tommaso M. *Dynare User Guide: An Introduction to the Solution & Estimation of DSGE Models*, June 2010.

Grossman, Gene M. and Elhanan Helpman. 2002a. "Outsourcing in a Global Economy." *NBER Working Papers* 8728. Accessed June 29, 2014. http://www.nber.org/papers/w8728.pdf.

———. 2002b. "Outsourcing Versus FDI in Industry Equilibrium." *NBER Working Papers* 9300. Accessed June 29, 2014. http://www.nber.org/papers/w9300.pdf.

Gurin, Joel. 2014. *Open Data Now*. McGaw-Hill Education.

Hanson, Gordon H., Raymond J. Mataloni, and Matthew J. Slaughter. 2003. "Vertical Production Networks in Multinational Firms." *NBER Working Papers*: 9723. Accessed June 29, 2014. http://www.nber.org/papers/w9723.pdf.

Harrison, Ann E. and Margaret S. McMillan. 2006. "Outsourcing Jobs? Multinationals and US Employment." *NBER Working Papers*: 12372. Accessed June 29, 2014. http://www.nber.org/papers/w12372.pdf.

Hayashi, Fumio and Edward C. Prescott. 2002. "The 1990s in Japan: A Lost Decade." *Review of Economic Dynamics* 5: 206–235. Accessed May 19, 2014. doi: 10.1006/redy.2001.0149.

Hirth, Matthias, Tobias Hoßfeld, and Phuoc Tran-Gia. 2013. "Analyzing Costs and Accuracy of Validation Mechanisms for Crowdsourcing Platforms." *Mathematical & Computer Modelling* 57, no. 11: 2918–2932. Accessed January 5, 2014. doi:10.1016/j.mcm.2012.01.006.

Hitt, Lorin M. 1999. "Information Technology and Firm Boundaries: Evidence from Panel Data." *Information Systems Research* 10, no. 2: 134–149.

Hitt, Lorin M. and Erik Brynjolfsson. 1997. "Information Technology and Internal Firm Organization: An Exploratory Analysis." *Journal of Management Information Systems* 14, no. 2: 81–101.

Hoffmann, Leah. 2012. "Data Mining Meets City Hall." *Communications of the ACM* 55, no. 6: 19–21.

Howe, Jeff. 2006. "Crowdsourcing: A Definition." Blog Post on June 2, 2006. Accessed February 7, 2014. http://www.crowdsourcing.com/cs/2006/06/crowdsourcing_a.html.

———. 2009. *Crowdsourcing: Why the Power of the Crowd is Driving the Future of Business.* Crown Business.

IDC. 2012. *Abstract, Worldwide SaaS and Cloud Software 2012–2016 Forecast* and *2011 Vendor Shares*, Accessed March 28, 2013. http://www.Idc.com/getdoc.Jsp?containerId=236184.

IPA. 2010. *IT Jinzai Hakusho 2010* (in Japanese). Accessed August 9, 2013. http://www.ipa.go.jp/files/000023694.pdf.

———. 2011. *IT Jinzai Hakusho 2011* (in Japanese). Accessed August 9, 2013. http://www.ipa.go.jp/files/000023691.pdf.

———. 2012. *IT Jinzai Hakusho 2012* (in Japanese). Accessed August 9, 2013. http://www.ipa.go.jp/files/000023689.pdf.

IT Strategic Headquarters. 2012. *Denshi Gyōsei Open Data Senryaku* (in Japanese). Accessed on April 6, 2014. http://www.kantei.go.jp/jp/singi/it2/denshigyousei.html.

Jansen, Wayne and Timothy Grance. 2011. *Guidelines on Security and Privacy in Public Cloud Computing*. National Institute of Standards and Technology, U.S. Department of Commerce. Accessed April 22, 2014. http://csrc.nist.gov/publications/nistpubs/800-144/SP800-144.pdf.

Jones, Randall S. and Taesik Yoon. 2008. "Enhancing the Productivity of the Service Sector in Japan." *OECD Economics Department Working Papers* 651.

Jorgenson, Dale W. 2002. *Economic Growth in the Information Age*. MIT Press.

Jorgenson, Dale W. and Kazuyuki Motohashi. 2003. "Economic Growth of Japan and the United States in the Information Age." *RIETI Discussion Paper Series* 03-E-015.

———. 2005. "Information Technology and the Japanese Economy." *Journal of the Japanese & International Economies* 19 (4): 460–481.

Jorgenson, Dale W. and Kevin J. Stiroh. 1999. "Information Technology and Growth." *American Economic Review* 89, no. 2: 109–115.

Jorgenson, Dale W., Mun S. Ho, and Jon D. Samuels. 2011. "Information Technology and U.S. Productivity Growth: Evidence from a Prototype Industry Production Account." *Journal of Productivity Analysis* 36, no. 2: 159–175. Accessed March 12, 2014. doi:10.1007/s11123-011-0229-z.

JSBRI. 2008. *White Paper on Small and Medium Enterprises in Japan 2008* (in Japanese). Japan Small Business Research Institute.

———. 2012. *White Paper on Small and Medium Enterprises in Japan 2012* (in Japanese). Japan Small Business Research Institute.

Keizai-Kikakucho. 2000. *IT Ka Ga Seisansei Ni Ataeru Kouka Ni Tsuite* (in Japanese). Accessed March 15, 2014. http://www5.cao.go.jp/2000/f/1031f-seisakukoka4.pdf.

Knight Foundation. 2013. *The Emergence of Civic Tech: Investments in a Growing Field*. Accessed April 22, 2014. http://www.knightfoundation.org/media/uploads/publication_pdfs/knight-civic-tech.pdf.

Kravis, Irving B. and Robert E. Lipsey. 1988. "Production and Trade in Services by U.S. Multinational Firms." *NBER Working Papers*: 2615. Accessed June 29, 2014. http://www.nber.org/papers/w2615.pdf.

Kydland, Finn E. and Edward C. Prescott. 1982. "Time to Build and Aggregate Fluctuations." *Econometrica* 50, no. 6: 1345–1370.

Liu, Runjuan and Daniel Trefler. 2008. "Much Ado about Nothing: American Jobs and the Rise of Service Outsourcing to China and India." *NBER Working Papers*: 14061. Accessed June 30, 2016. http://www.nber.org/papers/w14061.

Lloret, Elena, Laura Plaza, and Ahmet Aker. 2013. "Analyzing the Capabilities of Crowdsourcing Services for Text Summarization." *Language Resources & Evaluation* 47, no. 2: 337–369. Accessed January 5, 2014. doi:10.1007/s10579-012-9198-8.

Long, John B., Jr. and Charles I. Plosser. 1983. "Real Business Cycles." *Journal of Political Economy* 91, no. 1: 39–69.

Mandelman, Federico S. and Andrei Zlate. 2008. "Immigration and the Macroeconomy." *Federal Reserve Bank of Atlanta Working Paper* 25: 1–49.

Marjanovic, Sonja, Caroline Fry, and Joanna Chataway. 2012. "Crowdsourcing Based Business Models: In Search of Evidence for Innovation 2.0." *Science & Public Policy* 39, no. 3: 318–332. Accessed January 5, 2014. doi:10.1093/scipol/scs009.

Markusen, James. 2005. "Modeling the Offshoring of White-Collar Services: From Comparative Advantage to the New Theories of Trade and FDI." *NBER Working Papers*: 11827. Accessed June 29, 2014. http://www.nber.org/papers/w11827.pdf.

Markusen, James R., Anthony J. Venables, Denise Eby Konan, and Kevin H. Zhang. 1996. "A Unified Treatment of Horizontal Direct Investment, Vertical Direct Investment, and the Pattern of Trade in Goods and Services." *NBER Working Papers*: 5696. Accessed June 29, 2014. http://www.nber.org/papers/w5696.pdf.

Matsudaira, Jordan D. 1998. "The Return to Information Technology Investments in Japan." *Fujitsu Research Institute Economic Review* 2, no. 4: 43–57.

McNeill, Robert, Phil Fersht, and Tony Filippone. 2011. *What are Business Platforms and Why do They Represent the Future of Outsourcing?* HfS Research. Accessed April 22, 2014. http://www.horsesforsources.com/wp-content/uploads/2011/11/hfs-What-Are-Business-Platforms-why-are-they-the-future-of-Outsourcing.pdf.

Mell, Peter and Timothy Grance. 2011. *The NIST Definition of Cloud Computing*. National Institute of Standards and Technology. U.S. Department of Commerce. Accessed April 22, 2014. http://csrc.nist.gov/publications/nistpubs/800-145/SP800-145.pdf.

MIC. 2012. *Information and Communications in Japan White Paper 2012* (in Japanese). Ministry of Internal Affairs and Communications, Japan.

———. 2013. *Information and Communications in Japan White Paper 2013* (in Japanese). Ministry of Internal Affairs and Communications, Japan.

Michael, Boniface and Rashmi Michael. 2011. "A Transaction Cost Economics View of Outsourcing." *International Journal of Business, Humanities &*

Technology 1, no. 2: 34–43.
Milgrom, Paul R. and John Roberts. 1992. *Economics, Organization and Management*. Prentice-Hall.
Minetaki, Kazunori and Kiyohiko G. Nishimura. 2010. *Information Technology Innovation and the Japanese Economy*. Stanford University Press.
Mitra, Devashish and Priya Ranjan. 2007. "Offshoring and Unemployment." *NBER Working Papers*: 13149. Accessed June 29, 2014. http://www.nber.org/papers/w13149.pdf.
Miyazaki, Satoru, Hiroki Idota, and Hiroaki Miyoshi. 2012. "Corporate Productivity and the Stages of ICT Development." *Information Technology & Management* 13, no. 1: 17–26. Accessed April 22, 2014. doi:10.1007/s10799-011-0108-3.
Motohashi, Kazuyuki. 2003. "Firm Level Analysis of Information Network use and Productivity in Japan." *RIETI Discussion Paper 03-E-021*.
———. 2005. *IT Inobēshon no Jisshō Bunseki* (in Japanese). Tokyo: Tōyō Keizai Shinbunsha.
———. 2007. "Firm-Level Analysis of Information Network Use and Productivity in Japan." *Journal of the Japanese & International Economies* 21, no. 1: 121–137. doi:10.1016/j.jjie.2005.08.001.
Nakanishi, Yasuo and Tomohiko Inui. 2008. *"Kisei-Kanwa to Sangyō no Performance"* (in Japanese). In *Seisansei to Nihon-no Keizai Seichō*, edited by Kyoji Fukao and Tsutomu Miyagawa, 203–220: Tokyo Daigaku Shuppankai.
Nikkei Sangyo Shinbun. 2014. *"Chugoku 'Jinkai Nyuryoku' Kichi o miru, Gojiritsu ha 0.01% ika"* (in Japanese). May 8, 2014. Accessed May 19, 2014. http://www.nikkei.com/article/DGXNZO70830920X00C14A5X11000/.
Noguchi, Yukio. 1974. *Jōhō no Keizai Riron*. (in Japanese) Toyo Keizai Shinpō-Sha.
OECD. 2008. *OECD Recommendation of the Council for Enhanced Access and More Effective use of Public Sector Information* C(2008)36. Accessed April 22, 2014. http://www.oecd.org/internet/ieconomy/44384673.pdf.
Oliner, Stephen D. and Daniel E. Sichel. 1994. "Computers and Output Growth Revisited: How Big is the Puzzle?" *Brookings Papers on Economic Activity* (2): 273–334.
———. 2000. "The Resurgence of Growth in the Late 1990s: Is Information Technology the Story?" *Journal of Economic Perspectives* 14, no. 4: 3–22.
OMB. 2013. *Memorandum of the Heads of Executive Departments and Agencies*. Executive Office of the President, Office of Management and Budget.
Ono, Yukako and Victor Stango. 2005. "Outsourcing, Firm Size, and Product Complexity: Evidence from Credit Unions." *Economic Perspectives* 29, no. 1: 2–11.
Qaisar, Sara and Kausar Fiaz Khawaja. 2012. "Cloud Computing: Network Security Threats and Countermeasures." *Interdisciplinary Journal of Contemporary Research in Business* 3, no. 9: 1323–1329.

Reddy, V. Krishna and L. S. S. Reddy. 2011. "Security Architecture of Cloud Computing." *International Journal of Engineering Science & Technology* 3, no. 9: 7149–7155.

RIETI. 2009. *JIP 2009 Database,* Accessed July 10, 2011. http://www.rieti.Go.jp/jp/database/JIP2009/index.Html.

Rodriguez-Clare, Andres. 2007. "Offshoring in a Ricardian World." *NBER Working Papers*: 13203. Accessed June 29, 2014. http://www.nber.org/papers/w13203.pdf.

Ross, Peter. 2011. "How to Keep Your Head Above the Clouds: Changing ICT Worker Skill Sets in a Cloud Computing Environment." *Employment Relations Record* 11, no. 1: 62–74.

Schall, Daniel. 2013. "Automatic Quality Management in Crowdsourcing." *IEEE Technology & Society Magazine* 32, no. 4: 9–13. Accessed January 5, 2014. doi:10.1109/MTS.2013.2286420.

Seltzer, Ethan and Dillon Mahmoudi. 2013. "Citizen Participation, Open Innovation, and Crowdsourcing: Challenges and Opportunities for Planning." *Journal of Planning Literature* 28, no. 1: 3–18. Accessed January 5, 2014. doi:10.1177/0885412212469112.

Solow, Robert M. 1987. "We'd Better Watch Out." *New York Times Book Review*, July 12, 1987.

Sonoda, Shigeto. 2001. *Nihon kigyō Asia e: Kokusai shakaigaku no bouken.* (in Japanese). Yūhikaku.

Sørensen, Inge Ejbye. 2012. "Crowdsourcing and Outsourcing: The Impact of Online Funding and Distribution on the Documentary Film Industry in the UK." *Media, Culture & Society* 34, no. 6: 726–743. Accessed January 5, 2014. doi:10.1177/0163443712449499.

Strømmen-Bakhtiar, Abbas and Amir R. Razavi. 2011. "Should the "CLOUD" be Regulated? An Assessment." *Issues in Informing Science & Information Technology* 8: 219–230.

Sugo, Tomohiro and Kozo Ueda. 2008. "Estimating a Dynamic Stochastic General Equilibrium Model for Japan." *Journal of the Japanese and International Economies* 22, no. 4: 476–502. Accessed April 22, 2014. doi:10.1016/j.jjie.2007.09.002.

Tadelis, Steven and Oliver E. Williamson. 2013. "Transaction Cost Economics." In *Handbook of Organizational Economics*, edited by Robert Gibbons and John Roberts, 159–192: Princeton University Press.

Takagi, Soichiro. 2011. "Essays on the Globalization of Information Services and Japanese Economy." Master's Thesis, University of Tokyo.

———. 2012a. "Development of Open Data Policy in Europe" (in Japanese). *Journal of Information Processing and Management* 55, no. 10: 746–753.

———. 2012b. "*Oushu ni Okeru Open Data Seisaku Dōkō*" (in Japanese). *Administration & Information Systems* June: 72–76.

———. 2012c. "*Open Data no Shijō Kibo ni Semaru.*" (in Japanese). *Admin-*

istration & Information Systems, October, 71–75.

———. 2013. "Utilizing Open Data: 7. International Preparation for the Reuse of Data" (in Japanese). *Jōhō Shori* 54, no. 12: 1238–1243.

Takagi, Soichiro and Hideyuki Tanaka. 2010. "Academic Frontier of Globalization of IT-Service Industry: A Review from International and Spatial Economics Perspective." Paper presented at the annual meeting for the 29th Annual Conference of the Japan Association for Social and Economic Systems Studies, Kyoto, Kyoto, October 30–31.

———. 2011. "Globalization of Information Services and Industrial Structure of Japanese Economy." Paper presented at 10th International Conference of the Japan Economic Policy Association, Hyogo, November 19–20.

———. 2012a. "International Trade of Information Services, and Its Effect on Productivity and Industrial Structure in Japan." *Global Business & Economics Anthology* II: 334–345.

———. 2012b. "Offshore Outsourcing of Information Services and Its Effect on Productivity in Japan." *Journal of the Japan Association for Social and Economic Systems Studies* (33): 107–114.

———. 2012c. "Offshore Outsourcing of Information Services and Employment in Japan." *Journal of Economic Policy Studies* 9, no. 2: 29–32.

———. 2013a. "Information Technology and Modern Business Organization." Paper presented at the 12th International Conference of the Japan Economic Policy Association, Hokkaido, October 26–27.

———. 2014a. "Globalization of Information Services and the Industrial Structure of the Japanese Economy." *The Review of Socionetwork Strategies* 8, no. 1: 19–33. Accessed June 29, 2014. doi:10.1007/s12626-014-0041-0.

———. 2014b. "Macroeconomic Analysis of Cloud Computing." *Journal of Economic Policy Studies* 11, no. 2.

Takagi, Soichiro, Hideyuki Tanaka, and Shigeto Sonoda. 2011. "Foreign Direct Investment in Service Sector and National Culture." *Journal of Economic Policy Studies* 8, no. 2: 83–86.

Takemura, Toshihiko. 2003. "*Nihon Ginkō-Gyou ni Okeru Jōhō System Toushi to Seisansei Oyobi Kouritsusei.*" *RCSS Discussion Paper Series* 11.

Tamegawa, Kenichi, Yasuharu Ukai, and Ryokichi Chida. 2014. "Macroeconomic Contribution of the Cloud Computing System." *RISS Discussion Paper Series* 34.

Tapscott, Don and Anthony Williams. 2008. *Wikinomics*. Atlantic Books.

UK National Archives. 2009. *Criteria for Exceptions to Marginal Cost Pricing, December 2009*. Accessed April 22, 2014. http://www.Nationalarchives.gov.uk/documents/information-management/criteria-Exceptions-Marginal-Cost-Pricing.Pdf.

Ukai, Yasuharu. ed. 2005. *Economic Analysis of Information System Investment in Banking Industry.* Springer.

———. 2013. "Research Note: The Paradox of Cloud Computing in Japan."

The Review of Socionetwork Strategies 7, no. 1: 53–61.
Ukai, Yasuharu and Shintaro Inagaki. 2014. "Statistical Analysis of the Cloud Computing System and Financial Data at Japanese Enterprises." *RISS Discussion Paper Series* 33.
Ukai, Yasuharu and Toshihiko Takemura. 2001. "Panel Data Analysis of Computer Software Assets in the Bank of Japan: Estimation from the Financial Reports." *The Economic Review of Kansai University* 51, no. 3: 29–47.
Ukai, Yasuharu and Shinji Watanabe. 2001. "Information Technology Investment in Japanese Banks: Panel Data Analyses." *The Economic Review of Kansai University* 51, no. 2: 51–81.
Umezawa, Takashi. 2007. "The International Division of Labor in Software Industry : The Case Study of Japan and China" (in Japanese). *The Annual Bulletin, Japan Academy of International Business Studies* 13.
van Welsum, Desiree and Xavier Reif. 2006. "We can Work it Out – the Globalisation of ICT-Enabled Services." *NBER Working Paper 12799*. Accessed June 30, 2016. http://www.nber.org/papers/w12799.pdf.
Von Hippel, Eric. 2005. *Democratizing Innovation*. The MIT Press. Accessed April 22, 2014. http://evhippel.Mit.edu/books/.
Wakabayashi, Kei. 2013. "*Code for America, Civic Hacker ga Gyousei wo Kaeru*" (in Japanese). *Wired* (Japan Edition) 9: 96–102.
Walsh, Bryan. 2013. "Peace Corps for Geeks." *Time* 181, no. 14.
Watanabe, Shinji and Yasuharu Ukai. 2003. "Limit of Aggregate Level Analysis of Information System Investment." In *Economic Analysis of Information System Investment in Banking Industry*, edited by Yasuharu Ukai, 55–70: Springer.
Willcocks, Leslie P. and Mary C. Lacity. 1995. "Information Systems Outsourcing in Theory and Practice." Editorial, *Journal of Information Technology* 10: 203–207.
Williamson, Oliver E. 1983. *Markets and Hierarchies, Analysis and Antitrust Implications: A Study in the Economics of Internal Organization*. New York: Free Press.
Womack, Brian. 2013. "Facebook Market Value Tops $100 Billion Amid Mobile Push." *Bloomberg*, August 27. Accessed April 6, 2014. http://www.bloomberg.com/news/2013-08-26/facebook-Market-Value-Tops-100-Billion-Amid-Mobile-Ad-Push.html.

Index

A
AFM (acceptance foreign multinational cooperations)   62, 69
Amazon.com   119
 Amazon Mechanical Turk   32
 Amazon Web Services   114
Amiti, M.   25, 39, 95
Ang, S.   20
Apache   30
Arndt, S.   23
Arthur, W. B.   5
ASEAN6 countries   78, 80, 84, 88, 89, 92, 94, 103, 106, 107, 157
AsiaBarometer   60, 61, 62, 63, 153
Asian countries   13, 15, 26, 33, 106, 107, 109, 154

B
Bahli, B.   20
Baldwin, C. Y.   22
Bartel, A.   23
Bayrak, E.   29
Benkler, Y.   10
Berman, E.   23
Bills, S.   54
Biswas   21
Black, S. E.   19
Blair. M. M.   20
Botsman, R.   30
boundary of firms   19, 20
BPO (business process outsourcing)   78
BPR (business process re-engineering)   100, 102, 106
Brabham, D.   30, 32

Bresnahan, T.   4, 19
Bressand, A.   30, 150
bridge-SE   50
Brynjolfsson, E.   17, 18

C
call-center operation   3, 20, 37, 38, 50, 52, 53, 56
captive sourcing   48, 52
China   21, 24, 53, 54, 77, 78, 80, 84, 92, 93, 94, 103, 104, 105, 108, 122, 158
 environmental regulation   21
 regional condition   21
 inshoring from China   24
Civic Tech movement   144, 151
cloud computing   3, 7, 8, 9, 11, 13, 26, 28, 38, 50, 54, 55, 56, 93, 95, 114, 115, 118, 125, 139, 154, 156
 categories of cloud computing   38, 114
 international cloud computing   55
 organizational structure of cloud computing   55
 share of cloud computing   117
Coase, R.   40, 42, 146
Code for America   144
Code for Sapporo   144
cost effect   102
CRM (Customer Relationship Management)   39, 52, 53, 58, 114, 156
crowd-sourcing   8, 29, 30, 32,

175

139, 140
  definition of crowdsourcing 30
Cudanov, M.   28
cultural variables   61
Cusumano, M. A.   44
CWS (collaborative working spheres)   50

D
Data.gov.uk   141
Dibben, J.   20
Dropbox   113
DSD (distributed software development)   50
DSGE (Dynamic Stochastic General Equilibrium) analysis   5, 7, 9, 12, 26, 27, 28, 109, 115, 121, 128, 154, 157, 159, 160

E
employment   4, 12, 13, 15, 23, 24, 33, 79, 87, 92, 154
  outsourcing and employment in Japan   87, 94, 106, 108
  deployment cost   118
  downward pressure of employment   157
  unemployment   24
EMS (Electronic Manufacturing Services)   46
ENG (English fluency)   62, 66
EU countries   15, 24, 25, 27, 92, 108, 109, 142
Ex Ante Small Numbers   41

F
Falk, M.   24, 25, 39, 82, 92, 95
FDI   12, 21, 23, 24, 59, 61, 62, 63, 66, 69, 70, 107, 153, 154
  cultural factor on FDI   21
  FDI flow in China   22
Feenstra, R. C.   23, 82

financial processing   38
firm value   *see* productivity
Flextronics   46
Florida, R.   160
fluctuation of business cycle   26
FPT software   52
Frankrone, E. R.   32
Fujita, M.   159
Fukao, K.   107

G
Garicano, L.   146
GDP   27, 62, 66, 123, 125, 126, 127
GIS (Geographical Information System)   143
global R&D   21
globalization   30
Google   113, 119
  Google Apps   55
Griffoli, T. M.   115, 121
Grossman, G. M.   23, 24

H
Hanson, G. H.   23, 82
Harrison, A. E.   23
Helpman, E.   23, 24
heterogeneity of service economy   43, 44, 47, 48, 50, 56, 57, 153
Hitt, L. M.   17, 18
hold-up problems   41, 42
horizontal accumulation   13
host country   12
Howe, J.   30

I
IaaS (infrastructure as a service)   39
ICT   28, 77, 78
  ICT worker   28, 148
IM (instant messaging)   50
immigration   26
Inagaki, S.   28

Index 177

India 24, 78, 80, 84, 92, 93, 94, 106, 107
information services 10
  components of information services 79
  outsourcing of information services 11, 83
InnoCentive 32
inshoring 24
integrated approach 5
international trade agreements 21
Internet 17, 140
intra-firm management 4
Inui, T. 100, 101
Ireland 78
Israel 78
iStock photo 32
information technology (IT)
  IT investment 17, 120, 123
  IT stock 102, 103
  ITES (IT-enabled services) 59

J
Japan, Japanese economy 5, 13, 17, 25, 26, 32, 33, 39, 77, 78, 80, 82, 84, 92, 94, 106, 107, 114, 124, 139, 157
  Japanese firms 28, 29, 48, 55
  Japanese information services industry 18, 82
  Japanese MNCs 21
  GDP of Japan 123, 126
  open data in Japan 140
  use of Google Apps in Japan 55
Jones, R. S. 21, 107
Jorgenson, D. W. 17, 100, 118, 123

K
Kravis, I. B. 23
Kwon, H. U. 107

L
Lacity, M. C. 20
Linkdata.org 147
Linux 30
Lipsey, R. E. 23
Liu, R. 24, 39
Lloret, E. 32
Lynch, L. M. 19

M
M&A 52
macroeconomic framework 19, 113
manufacturing sector 25, 89, 92, 107, 108
Markusen, J. R. 22, 24
mass collaboration 3, 7, 9, 29, 30, 32, 139, 145, 149, 150, 155, 156
  bottom-up collaboration 146
  principles of mass collaboration 29
McMillan, M. S. 23
McNeil, R. 54
Michael, B. 20
micro-foundation 26
Microsoft 46, 119
Milgrom, P. R. 38
Minetaki, K. 18, 107
Mitra, D. 22, 24
MNCs 21, 60, 61, 62, 69
Moshi Moshi Hotline 53
Motohashi, K. 17, 100, 123, 124
Mozilia 30

N
Nakanishi, Y. 100, 101
national culture 12, 21

Index

regional characteristics 13
nationalism / internationalism 63
networked production 160
Nishimura, K. G. 18, 107, 108
Noguchi, Y. 10, 149
non-OECD countries 85, 88, 89, 92, 103

O

OECD countries 80, 84, 88, 90, 92, 107
OEM (Original Equipment Manufacturer) 46
offshore outsourcing 15, 38, 40, 77
    empirical analysis on the offshore outsourcing 22, 26, 77
    theoretical themes on offshoring 24
Oliner, S. D. 17
OLS analysis 62, 66
online encyclopedia 8
Ono, Y. 20
open data movement 8, 13, 139, 140, 144, 150
    principles of open data 141
    open data movement in Japanese local communities 140, 142, 143, 144, 147, 149
Open Knowledge Foundation 142, 143
open source software 8
organization 3, 4, 19
    hierarchical organization 29, 48, 156
    organizational change 5, 7, 15
    organizational structure, latest developments 12
    vertical organizational disintegration 156

OSS (open source software) 141, 146, 149
outsourcing of information services 3, 5, 37, 83, 87, 102, 153
    Japan's offshore outsourcing of information services 88
    outsourcing decision 45
    types of outsourcing 37

P

PaaS (Platform as a Service) 39
PAM (personal activity management) 50
peer production 140
Philippines 78, 80
POC (pride of own contry) 62, 66, 69
productivity 4, 12, 13, 15, 15, 17, 27, 33, 99, 100, 118, 120, 122, 124, 125, 129, 154
    productivity at firm level 19
    productivity in Japan 25, 100, 106, 108
    productivity paradox 17, 123

R

R&D (research and development) 22, 78, 79, 80, 92, 94, 107, 108, 109
    global R&D 21
Ranjan, P. 22, 24
RBC (real business cycle) 26, 115
regional characteristics 13
Rivard, S. 20
Robert-Nicoud, F. 22
Roberts, J. 38
Rodriguez-Clare, A. 22
Rogers, R. 30
Ross, P. 28

S

SaaS (Software as a service)   38, 114
Salesforce.com   114, 117, 119
security problems   49
service and information-centric economy   10, 11
   service economy   43
service attributes   43, 46, 57
service sector   44, 59
   international production sharing of service sector   12
   offshore outsourcing of service sector   12
Sichel, D. E.   17
simultaneous production and consumption of service economy   43, 44, 47, 48, 49, 50, 52, 53, 56, 57, 153
Singapore   93
skilled labor   23, 24, 94
SME (small and medium size enterprises)   27, 119
software development   3, 7, 11, 30, 37, 38, 50, 56, 93, 94
   in Japan   51
Stango, V.   20
Stiroh, K. J.   17
Straub, D. W.   20

T

Takagi, S.   25, 39, 82, 89
Takemura, T.   18
Tamegawa, K.   28
Tanaka, H.   25, 39, 82, 89
Tapscott, D.   29, 30, 140, 146
TCE (Transaction Cost Economics) analysis   8, 9, 11, 20, 40, 42, 47, 150, 155
   analytical tool   47, 50, 57
technological architecture   26, 113

technological change   37
TFP (Total Factor Productivity)   17, 25, 99, 100, 101, 102, 103, 106, 107, 108, 113, 123, 127, 128, 129
Threadless.com   32
TOC (technology oriented culture)   62
traditional outsourcing   82, 83, 102
transaction costs   37, 57, 156, *see* TCE
Trefler, D.   24, 39
TV conferencing   50

U

Ukai, Y.   17, 18, 28
United Kingdom   23, 26, 95, 140, 142
   UK Employment   23, 25
United States   15, 21, 22, 23, 24, 26, 39, 78, 80, 84, 92, 99, 107, 108, 109, 140, 141
   cloud computing in U. S.   39
   global R&D investments of U. S.   21
   employment in U.S.   25
   US wages   25

V

Van Zandt, T.   146
Vietnam   52, 53, 78, 80
virtualization   54

W

wage gap   22
Watanabe, S.   17, 18
Wei S.-J.   25, 39, 95
Wikinomics   140
Wikipedia   30, 32
Willcocks, L. P.   20
Williams, A.   29, 30, 140, 146

Williamson, O. E.   40, 41, 42, 61
Wolfmayr   24, 25, 39, 82, 92, 95

Y
Y2K issue   88
Yoon, T.   107